Crazy About Crockery!

101 Easy and Inexpensive Recipes for Less than .75¢ a serving

Penny E. Stone

Crazy About Crockery

101 Quick, Easy & Inexpensive Recipes for Less than .75 Cents a Serving

Penny E. Stone

Also by Penny E. Stone

CRAZY ABOUT CROCKERY: 101 Soup & Stew Recipes for
Less than .75 cents a serving

CRAZY ABOUT CROCKERY: 101 Recipes for Entertaining
at Less than .75 cents a serving

CRAZY ABOUT CROCKERY: 101 Easy & Inexpensive
Recipes for Less than .75 cents a serving

365 Quick, Easy & Inexpensive Dinner Menus

CHAMPION PRESS, LTD.
FREDONIA, WISCONSIN
www.championpress.com

ISBN 1-891400-12-6 ~ LCCN 2002103113
Manufactured in Canada 10 9 8 7 6 5 4
Book Design by Kathy Campbell, Wildwood Studios

Introduction

COOKING WITH A SLOW COOKER CAN SAVE YOU time, money and energy! With all these benefits its no wonder we have seen a return of the slow cooker. Thousands of homecooks are pulling their dusty pots from storage and discovering the many benefits of putting the slow cooker back on the counter!

Once thought of as a contraption for only concocting soups and stews, the way we view the slow cooker has changed. This book will help you expand your repertoire of recipes that can be prepared in this quick and easy tool.

On the average it takes about 10-20 minutes prep time to assemble your ingredients and fill your slow cooker. Then simply turn on your slow cooker and go about your day!

There's even more benefits than the ease of preparation. Cooking with a slow cooker can help you save money in three ways: 1. It costs less to operate a slow cooker for 8 hours than it does to heat your oven for 1 hour. 2. You can use less expensive cuts of meat and still end up with moist and tender results. 3. Recipes calling for meat can be stretched by using other ingredients and less meat, thus making your grocery dollar stretch farther.

The following recipes are ones I use to feed my family of 5 for a cost per serving of 75-cents or less! Each recipe has a per serving cost that is estimated and based on the sale prices I pay in central Indiana. Your cost of living or sale prices may be higher or lower than mine, so each cost is only an estimate.

Enough of me touting the many benefits of slow cooker cooking. You are about to see for yourself the various ways a slow cooker can revolutionize the way you cook and the way you eat.

SECTION I

One-Pot Meals

With a slow cooker, you can prepare complete meals without fuss, hassle, or expense! You don't have to worry about staggering the times you add ingredients.... just throw all of them in at once. Not only will everything cook perfectly, but all the flavors will blend making your meal even more enticing. The following recipes are designed to feed a family of 6 and with the cost per serving at .75-cents or less. That means each "slow cooker meal" costs under $5.00!!! Where else can you feed a family of 6 for $5.00 or less?

One-Pot Beef Meals

◦ EASY SLOW COOKER STEAK MEAL

Prep. Time: 15 minutes • Serves 6 • Cost: about 73-cents per serving

2-3 lbs. round steak, cut in ½ -inch strips
1 large or 2 medium onions, sliced thin with rings separated
6-8 medium potatoes, peeled and cubed
2 cans French-styled green beans, drained
1 can tomato soup
¼ cup water
2 tablespoons steak sauce
2 teaspoons Worcestershire sauce
1 (1 lb.) can tomatoes, chopped
Garlic salt
Salt and pepper

Before cutting round steak into strips, sprinkle the garlic salt, table salt, and pepper liberally over both sides of the meat. Cut into strips. Arrange meat in slow cooker. In separate container, combine condensed tomato soup with ¼ cup water, steak sauce, Worcestershire sauce and chopped tomatoes. Stir to mix well and pour mixture over meat strips. Arrange onion slices over meat. Add potatoes and top with drained green beans. Cover with lid and cook on high for 6-8 hours.

PENNY'S GARDEN MEDLEY ROAST WITH POTATOES

Prep. Time: 5 minutes • Serves: 6+ • Cost: about 75-cents per serving

1 (3-4 lb.) beef round/top round roast
2 pints Garden Medley sauce (see page 82)
   or substitute 1 quart V-8® tomato juice plus:
   2 teaspoons basil
   1 teaspoon oregano
   ½ teaspoon Rosemary
   ½ teaspoon thyme
   ½ teaspoon celery salt
   1 teaspoon garlic powder
   2 teaspoons onion flakes
   2 teaspoons beef seasoning or beef bouillon
   1 teaspoon seasoned salt
   ¼ teaspoon black pepper
1 quart green beans, drained
6-8 medium potatoes, peeled

Trim roast of all visible fat. Put meat in slow cooker and add peeled potatoes and green beans. Add Garden Medley sauce. Cover with lid and cook on high for 7 hours.

Hungarian Round Steak

Prep. Time: about 10 minutes • Servings: 6 • Cost: about 69-cents per serving

2-3 lb. lean round steak, cut into serving portions
2 large onions, chopped
1 clove garlic, minced
2 quarts canned tomatoes
½ cup flour
2 teaspoons unseasoned meat tenderizer, opt.*
1 teaspoon salt
½ teaspoon coarse black pepper
1 teaspoon paprika
½ teaspoon dried thyme
1 bay leaf

Combine flour with unseasoned meat tenderizer in a baggie. Place each piece of meat in baggie and shake to evenly coat each piece with flour. Place floured meat in slow cooker. Add onions and garlic. Open tomatoes and with a knife, cut up tomatoes before pouring in to slow cooker. Add seasonings. Cover with lid and cook on high for 6 hours. Remove bay leaf before serving. The tomato-based sauce makes an excellent gravy over cooked noodles or rice.

*Optional: If you don't use meat tenderizer then reduce heat to low and increase cooking time to 9 hours.

Safe Food Storage

To avoid the possibility of food poisoning, don't store leftover food in your slow cooker. Always transfer slow cooker contents to a suitable container and refrigerate or freeze immediately after serving.

For slow cookers that have removable crocks, always place the hot crock on either a hot pad or trivet to protect your table or counter surface from blistering from the heat. Also, don't take a hot crock and put it directly in the refrigerator. You run the risk of cracking the crock with the drastic change in temperature.

DRIED BEEF 'N' MAC

Prep. Time: about 20 minutes • Servings: 6 • Cost: about 68-cents per serving

2 small or 1 large container dried beef, cut in strips
2 cups shredded cheddar cheese
1 cup shredded Colby cheese
1 onion, finely chopped
1 small jar pimento, drained and cut up
2 cans cream of mushroom soup
2 soup cans milk
2 cups uncooked elbow macaroni
6 hard boiled eggs, chopped
2 cups frozen peas

Combine soup and milk in slow cooker. Stir to blend well. Add dried beef, onion, pimento, boiled eggs and frozen peas. Cover with lid and cook on high for 4 hours. Add remaining ingredients and stir to blend well. Cover with lid and continue cooking for another 1-2 hours. Stir before serving.

Pepper Steak

Prep. Time: 15-20 minutes • Servings: 6+ • Cost: about 71-cents per serving

2 to 3 lbs. round steak
1 cup water
¼ teaspoon garlic powder
1 tablespoon cornstarch
2 tablespoons butter, melted
2 tablespoons soy sauce
2 beef bouillon cubes
1 large green pepper, cut into strips
¼ teaspoon coarse black pepper

Combine melted butter and water in slow cooker. Stir in garlic powder, cornstarch, soy sauce, beef bouillon cubes and black pepper. Add green pepper strips. Cut meat into thin strips about 2 inches long by ¼ inch wide. Add meat to slow cooker. Cover with lid and let cook for 6-8 hours. Serve plain or over cooked rice or noodles.

Corned Beef Casserole

Prep. Time: 10 minutes • Servings: 4-5 • Cost: about 69-cents per serving

1 can (12 oz) corned beef, chopped
¼ lb. American cheese, cubed
2 cans cream of mushroom soup
1 soup can water
1 cup milk
1 medium to large onion, chopped
4 cups cubed potatoes, raw
1-2 cups sliced carrots
1 cup sliced mushrooms, optional
1 cup buttered crumbs or croutons

Combine all ingredients in slow cooker and stir to blend well. Turn setting on high and cover with lid. Cook on high for 6-8 hours.

Brown Gravy Beef Roast with Vegetables

Prep. Time: about 10 minutes • Serves: 6+ • Cost: about 72-cents per serving

1 (3-5 lb.) beef roast, trimmed of visible fat
2 packets brown gravy mix
2 cups water
6-9 medium potatoes, peeled and halved
4-6 large carrots, cut in pieces
1 onion, sliced
1 cup fresh sliced mushrooms, optional
1 teaspoon salt
½ teaspoon black pepper

Set meat in slow cooker and sprinkle with salt. Arrange vegetables around meat. In saucepan, prepare gravy mixes with water according to package directions. Pour over meat and vegetables. Sprinkle salt and pepper over vegetables. Cover with lid and cook on high for 7-9 hours.

One-Pot Chicken Meals

A TASTE OF THE ORIENT

Prep. Time: 12 minutes • Servings: 6 • Cost: about 71-cents per serving

2 cups diced chicken (canned or cooked)
2 stalks celery, diced
1 large sweet onion, diced
1 green pepper, diced
1 can water chestnuts, drained and chopped
1 can bean sprouts, drained
1 tablespoon soy sauce
2 cups uncooked instant rice
3 cups water, boiling
2 pkgs. Ramen™ noodles, chicken flavored

In boiling water, dissolve the chicken flavoring packets found in the Ramen noodles packages. Pour into slow cooker. With your hands, break the uncooked Ramen noodles into pieces. Add those to the slow cooker. Add all remaining ingredients and stir to blend well. Cover with lid and cook on high for 6 hours. Top each serving with chow mein or rice noodles, if desired.

CRUNCHY CHICKEN AND MUSHROOMS ❀

Prep. Time: 10 minutes • Servings: 5-6 • Cost: about 69-cents per serving

5-6 chicken thighs or breasts, skin removed
    (1 per person)
1 onion, finely chopped
2 cans cream of chicken soup
1 soup can water
2 cups sliced mushrooms
2 stalks celery, diced
1 can water chestnuts, drained and sliced
2 cups chow mein noodles, optional

Combine soups with water, onion, mushrooms, celery, and water chestnuts. Stir to blend well. Set chicken in slow cooker and spoon soup mixture over each piece. Cover with lid and cook on high for 6-7 hours. Top with chow mein noodles, if desired, when ready to serve.

OLD MEXICO CHICKEN

Prep. Time: 15-20 minutes • Servings: 6 • Cost: about 74-cents per serving

1 whole chicken, cut up as for frying, skin removed
1 (1 lb.) can whole tomatoes
1 large onion, chopped
2 garlic cloves, chopped
½ cup fresh parsley, chopped, or 2 tablespoons dried parsley
½ cup seedless raisins
½ cup blanched almonds
½ cup pitted black olives, chopped or sliced
1 cup mild banana peppers, chopped or sliced
1 jalapeno pepper, seeds & stem removed, left whole
¼ cup cooking sherry
3 tablespoons oil
1 teaspoon salt
½ teaspoon black pepper

Wash and skin chicken. Add all ingredients to slow cooker. Cover with lid and cook on high for 6-8 hours. Sauce is good served over cooked rice.

Making Perfect Meat

When cooking meats in the slow cooker with the intention of using the broth as either a soup base or broth, you'll want to transfer the liquid to a suitable container and refrigerate it so the fat will separate from the rest of the broth. Once the fat congeals at the top, it can easily be removed and discarded. Reheat gelled broth and continue with your recipe. If you're planning to make chicken and noodles or some other chicken based broth, always add about a teaspoon or two of the separated fat back to the gelled liquid. This will produce a richer, fuller tasting soup base or stock.

Chicken 'n' Stuffing

Prep. Time: 15-20 minutes • Servings: 6+ • Cost: about 73-cents per serving

1 whole chicken fryer, skin removed, cut up
3 cups water
2 teaspoons salt
½ teaspoon pepper
2 cans cream of chicken soup
2 stalks celery, sliced
1 can peas, drained, or 2 cups frozen peas
1 cup shredded cheddar cheese
2 cups Pepperidge Farm® Herb Stuffing Mix

Place chicken in slow cooker. Add water, salt, pepper, and celery. Cover with lid and cook on high for 5-7 hours. Remove meat from slow cooker and let cool. Add all remaining ingredients and stir to blend well. Pick chicken off bone and return meat to slow cooker in bite-sized pieces. Cover with lid and reduce temperature to low, let cook for 1-2 additional hours.

ALMOND CLASSIC CHICKEN

Prep. Time: 15-20 minutes • Servings: 6 • Cost: about 70-cents per serving

1 whole chicken, cut up, skin removed
2 cups water
1 large onion, chopped
1 teaspoon salt
½ to ¾ teaspoon black pepper, depending upon taste
3 stalks celery, diced
1 pkg. (10 oz) frozen peas, thawed
1 can (4 oz.) sliced mushrooms, drained
2 tablespoons cornstarch
½ cup water
½ teaspoon ground ginger
3 tablespoons soy sauce
½ to 1 cup toasted slivered almonds

Arrange chicken pieces in slow cooker. Scatter chopped onion and celery over the meat. Sprinkle with ½ teaspoon salt. Add 1½ cups water. Cover with lid and cook on high for 5 hours. Remove chicken from slow cooker and set aside to cool. To the remaining juices, add thawed peas and mushrooms. Dissolve cornstarch in ½ cup cold water and pour into slow cooker. Add all remaining ingredients. Pick chicken off bone and tear into bite-sized pieces. Add meat to slow cooker and stir to blend well. Cover with lid and reduce heat to low. Continue cooking for 2 hours on the low setting to allow flavors to blend. Serve over cooked rice.

COLORFUL CHEDDAR CHICKEN

Prep. Time: 15 minutes Servings: 6+ Cost: about 74-cents per serving

1 whole chicken, cut up, skin removed
1 cup water
8 slices dried bread, torn in pieces
½ cup chopped celery
1 onion, chopped or 6-8 green onions, chopped
½ cup mayonnaise
½ cup green pepper, chopped
1 small can pimentos, chopped and drained
2 cups shredded sharp cheddar cheese
1 can cream of mushroom soup
1 soup can of water
1 cup chopped carrot

Rub each piece of chicken with mayonnaise. Combine chicken, water, celery, onion, green pepper, and carrot in slow cooker, Cover with lid and cook 6-7 hours. Remove chicken and add all remaining ingredients to slow cooker. Stir to blend well. Return chicken to slow cooker. Cover and continue cooking for another 1-2 hours.

Fish

CHEESY TUNA & RICE

Prep. Time: 10 minutes • Servings: 6+ • Cost: about 68-cents per serving

1 can cream of celery soup
1 can cream of mushroom soup
2 1/3 cups water
1 teaspoon salt
1 tablespoon dried minced onion
2 1/3 cups uncooked instant rice
2 cups frozen peas
2 cans (6 oz) tuna, drained & flaked
½ cup Cheese Whiz®
4 slices American cheese
1 cup shredded cheddar cheese
¼ teaspoon pepper

Combine both cans of soup with water in slow cooker. Add salt, onion, peas, tuna, Cheese Whiz® and the 4 slices of American cheese. Cover with lid and cook on high for 2 hours. When mixture is hot and cheeses have melted, stir in rice and pepper. Cover and reduce heat to low. Cook for another hour and then serve.

Tuna Potluck

Prep. Time: about 13 minutes • Servings: 4-6 • Cost: about 60-cents per serving

2 cans (6 oz) tuna, drained
1 can evaporated milk
2 tablespoons cornstarch dissolved in ¼ cup water
5-8 med. white potatoes, peeled and diced
1 cup shredded cheddar cheese
4 slices American processed cheese
1 small pkg. (3 oz.) cream cheese
1 bunch (6-10) green onions, chopped
1 jar (2 oz.) pimento, chopped
½ cup milk
2 eggs, beaten
1 teaspoon salt
Dash nutmeg

Combine all ingredients in slow cooker. Stir to blend well. Cover and cook on low for 4-5 hours. Serve with sliced tomatoes.

Chipped Tuna Pot

Prep. Time: about 8 minutes • Servings: 4-6 • Cost: about 65-cents per serving

2 cans (6 oz.) chunk tuna, drained & flaked
1 can peas, drained, or 2 cups frozen peas, thawed
1 cup sliced or chopped celery
1 small to medium sweet onion, chopped
2 large carrots, grated
1 can cream of mushroom soup
1½ cups milk
1 bag of potato chips, crushed

Add all ingredients except potato chips to slow cooker. Stir to blend well. Cook on low for 3-4 hours. Add crushed chips and stir to mix well. Serve immediately.

Pork

"BAKED" PORK CHOPS AND POTATOES

Prep. Time: about 10 minutes • Servings: 6 • Cost: about 75-cents per serving

6 pork chops, trimmed of excess fat, bones removed
1 medium green pepper, diced
6-9 potatoes, peeled and sliced
1-2 onions, chopped, depending upon taste
2 teaspoons salt
1 can tomato soup
1 soup can water
1 tablespoon Worcestershire sauce

Sprinkle both sides of chops with 1 teaspoon of salt. Set aside. Slice potatoes and put them in the slow cooker. Add the green pepper and chopped onions. Toss to evenly distribute. Sprinkle remaining teaspoon of salt over potatoes and vegetables. Lay pork chops on top of potatoes. In separate container, combine soup with water and Worcestershire sauce. Stir to mix well and evenly pour over chops. Cover with lid and cook on high for 7-9 hours.

❧ LAYERED PORK MEAL

Prep. Time: about 15 minutes • Servings: 6 • Cost: about 75-cents per serving

6 lean pork chops, steaks, or cutlets; bones & fat removed
1 teaspoon salt
1 teaspoon seasoned salt
½ teaspoon black pepper
1 can cream of mushroom soup
1 can cream of celery soup
2 soup cans water
6-9 potatoes, peeled and sliced
4 carrots, peeled and sliced
2 stalks celery, sliced
2 onions, chopped

In bottom of slow cooker, layer sliced carrots. Next, add sliced celery. Place 3 pieces of pork on top of celery. Top with potatoes. Add a layer of chopped onions. Add remaining pork on top of onions. In a separate container, combine soups, water, salt, seasoned salt, and pepper. Stir soup mixture to blend well and pour over the top of all layers. Cover with lid and cook on high for 7-9 hours.

Kielbasa and Zucchini

Prep. Time: about 10 minutes • Servings: 4-6 • Cost: about 69-cents per serving

1-2 lbs. Kielbasa, cut in bite-sized pieces
2 medium to large zucchini, washed and diced
1 onion, diced
1 can stewed tomatoes
½ cup Parmesan cheese
½ teaspoon garlic powder
¼ teaspoon black pepper
1 cup shredded mozzarella cheese
1 teaspoon salt

Combine all ingredients in slow cooker except for mozzarella cheese. Stir to blend well. Cover with lid and cook on high for 4-5 hours. Add mozzarella cheese and let cheese melt before serving.

DEPRESSION POTLUCK

Prep. Time: about 10 minutes • Servings: 4-6 • Cost: about 58-cents per serving

1 pkg. (1 lb.) pork hot dogs, sliced in 1-inch chunks
2 cans pork and beans
1 large onion, chopped
¾ cup ketchup
½ cup water
1/3 cup vinegar
2 teaspoons dry mustard
½ teaspoon black pepper
1 teaspoon salt

Combine all ingredients in slow cooker. Stir to blend well. Cover with lid and cook on high for 5 hours.

 ## Slow Cooker Repairs

If your slow cooker lid or removable crock breaks, don't throw away the entire slow cooker unit! Instead, order the parts you need directly from your slow cooker manufacturer. Simply do an internet search or call your local retailer and ask for the manufacturer's contact information.

Sometimes slow cookers with removable crocks will have spill-overs that drip down the sides and stain the heating element shell. Be sure to check for any spill-overs when removing the crock. If you do have some, let the heating element cool completely. Then with a damp plastic scrub pad, clean up the spill. The best way to prevent spill-overs is to make sure you don't fill the slow cooker too full or use too much liquid for what is being cooked.

Cajun Beans 'n' Sausage

Prep. Time: about 12 minutes • Servings: 4-6 • Cost: about 69-cents per serving

1-2 lbs. smoked sausage, sliced

3 cans (15.5 oz.) red kidney beans, drained

2 cloves garlic, minced

1 medium green pepper, chopped

1 large onion, chopped

4 cups water

2 cups brown or long-grain rice (don't use instant)

1 teaspoon hot sauce

1 teaspoon Cajun seasoning

½ teaspoon red pepper, optional

Combine all ingredients in slow cooker. Stir to blend well. Cover with lid and cook on high for 6 hours.

◦ Pork Roast with Vegetables

Prep. Time: about 10 minutes • Serves: 6+ • Cost: about 49-cents per serving

1 (3-4 lbs.) pork roast, leave fat intact
1 onion, quartered or sliced
6-9 medium potatoes, peeled
4-6 large carrots, cut in thirds
2 packets brown or pork gravy mix
2 cups water
Salt and pepper

Set meat in slow cooker with fat side on top. Arrange vegetables around meat. In saucepan, prepare gravy packets with water according to package directions. Pour gravy over meat and vegetables. Salt and pepper meat and vegetables. Cover with lid and cook on high for 7-9 hours.

Pork Roast A La Carte

Prep. Time: about 10 minutes • Serves: 6 • Cost: about 52-cents per serving

1 (3-5 lbs.) pork roast, fat left intact
2 cups V-8® juice
8-12 small to medium red potatoes, skins left on
2 small onions, chopped or sliced
1 green pepper, sliced
2 cups fresh mushrooms, left whole or sliced in halves
1 teaspoon salt
½ teaspoon celery seed
1 teaspoon dried basil
½ teaspoon thyme

Set meat in slow cooker with fat side on top. Arrange vegetables around meat. Pour V-8® juice over slow cooker contents. Sprinkle with salt and seasonings. Cover with lid and cook on high for 7-9 hours.

Don't Crack the Crock

Protect your crock from cracking by not placing frozen meats and other food items directly against the interior surface. Always thaw frozen foods before placing them in the slow cooker. You can "fudge" on this rule just a bit by adding a frozen food to the middle of a soup, stew, or casserole as long as the food touching the interior surface is not frozen.

SECTION II

Casseroles

Casseroles in the slow cooker make satisfying meals that are easy to put together and cost effective for stretching your food budget. Even if you have picky eaters (like I do), you can either "hide" vegetables or make substitutions without too much trouble. The way I hide vegetables is to go ahead and cook them, then puree them and add the puree to the stock, sauce, or gravy. Another way is to chop them so small they're unrecognizable when they're cooked. When asked "what's those green flakes?" I simply reply "seasoning." These casserole recipes will feed 6 and the cost per serving is based on .75-cents or less per serving.

Beef Casseroles

"Souper" Beef Stroganoff

Prep. Time: about 15 minutes • Servings: 6 • Cost: about 72-cents per serving

1 lb. or more beef round steak
1 can cream of mushroom soup
1 can cream of celery soup
1 can cream of potato or onion soup
2 teaspoons beef seasoning mix or 3 beef bouillon cubes
1 cup water
½ cup flour
1 teaspoon salt
¼ teaspoon black pepper
1 pkg. egg noodles, prepared according to package directions

Combine salt and pepper with flour. Cut meat into strips or bite-sized pieces. Coat meat with flour and brown all sides in a little bit of oil. Transfer meat to slow cooker when beef has browned. Add soups and stir together. Cover with lid and cook on low for 6-8 hours. When ready to serve, prepare one package of egg noodles according to package directions, and drain. Add a small carton of sour cream to slow cooker mixture. Serve over cooked egg noodles.

PENNY'S BEEF STROGANOFF

Prep. Time: about 20 minutes • Servings: 6 • Cost: about 70-cents per serving

2 - 3 lbs. boneless round steak
2 teaspoons salt
¼ cup butter
¼ cup water
½ pint sour cream (may use light or fat free)
1 tablespoon dried chopped parsley
1 tablespoon dried chopped chives
6 green onions, chopped (tops included)
1 clove garlic, split in half
3 tablespoons flour
¼ teaspoon coarse black pepper
1 cup fresh sliced mushrooms
2 cans cream of mushroom soup
1 pkg. egg noodles, prepared according to package directions

Rub both sides of meat with garlic, then cut into thin slices (2 inches long x ¼ inch wide). In a baggie, combine flour, salt and pepper; toss meat strips with flour mixture, coating each piece well. In large skillet, melt butter with garlic halves. Add beef strips and cook over medium high heat until browned on all sides. Add onions and mushrooms and brown, cooking those for about 5 minutes. In slow cooker, combine water and soup; stir to blend. Add browned meat, chopped green onion, and mushroom slices. (Discard garlic halves.) Cover with lid and cook on high for 6 hours. Prepare noodles according to package directions. Just before serving, add sour cream to meat mixture and stir to blend well. Spoon meat mixture over cooked noodles and serve immediately.

E-Z VEGETABLE LASAGNA

Prep. Time: about 20 minutes • Servings: 6 • Cost: about 69-cents per serving

1 lb. lean ground beef or turkey
1 lb. skinless, smoked sausage, sliced
2 jars or cans prepared spaghetti sauce
2 cups water
4 medium zucchini, peeled and sliced (may substitute
    2-3 eggplant instead of zucchini)
3 cups ricotta cheese
1 egg
1 teaspoon parsley
2 teaspoons basil
2 teaspoons oregano
1 tablespoon Italian seasonings
½ teaspoon black pepper
2 cups shredded mozzarella cheese

In skillet, cook ground meat until browned. Drain and crumble
meat into slow cooker. In ricotta, stir in egg and seasonings. Add
all remaining ingredients to slow cooker and stir in seasoned
ricotta cheese. Cover with lid and cook on low for 5 hours.
Sprinkle mozzarella over each serving.

Beef 'n' Beans

Prep. Time: about 15-20 minutes • Servings: 5-6 • Cost: about 59-cents per serving

1 lb. lean ground beef
2 cans (16 oz.) pork 'n' beans
2 tablespoons brown sugar
¾ cup prepared BBQ sauce
1 onion, finely chopped
1 teaspoon salt
1 can refrigerated biscuits - 10 count, prepared according to package
    directions
2 cups shredded cheddar cheese

Brown meat and onion together, drain. In slow cooker, combine cooked beef, pork 'n' beans, brown sugar, BBQ sauce, and salt. Stir to blend well. Cover with lid and cook on high for 6 hours. Prepare biscuits according to package directions. For each serving, open two biscuits and scoop beef 'n' beans over biscuits. Cover each serving with shredded cheddar cheese. Let each serving set for 3-5 minutes before serving to allow cheese to melt.

BEEF 'N' ZUCCHINI

Prep. Time: about 20 minutes • Servings: 6 • Cost: about 55-cents per serving

1 lb. lean ground beef
4 cups cubed zucchini
2 tablespoons dried minced onion
1 teaspoon garlic powder
1 teaspoon salt
2 cups uncooked instant rice
3 cups tomato juice
2 tablespoons prepared mustard

In skillet, brown beef with minced onion. Cook until done. Drain off all grease. Crumble meat into slow cooker. Wash zucchini. Peeling zucchini is optional. Cut off both ends. Cube zucchini and add to slow cooker. Add all remaining ingredients. Stir to blend well. Cover with lid and cook on high for a minimum of 3 hours.

Beef and Cabbage Casserole

Prep. Time: about 20 minutes • Servings: 6 • Cost: about 67-cents per serving

1½ lbs. lean ground beef
1 large onion, chopped
½ green pepper, chopped
1 small head cabbage, coarsely chopped
2 cans tomato soup
1 soup can water
1 teaspoon salt
½ teaspoon pepper
1½ cups uncooked instant rice
1 teaspoon dried parsley flakes
½ teaspoon chives

In skillet, cook ground beef with chopped onion and green pepper added. When meat is cooked, drain off all grease. Crumble meat and vegetables into slow cooker. Add cabbage and rice. In a separate container, combine soup, water, salt, and seasonings. Stir to blend well and then pour into slow cooker. Stir to coat meat and vegetables. Cover with lid and cook on low for 4-6 hours.

TRADITIONAL STUFFED PEPPERS

Prep. Time: about 25 minutes • Serves: 6 • Cost: about 64-cents per serving

6 green peppers
1 ½ - 2 lbs. lean ground beef or turkey
1 onion, chopped
1 pint stewed tomatoes, cut up
1 cup water
1 tablespoon Worcestershire sauce
1 teaspoon black pepper
2 cups uncooked instant rice
2 cups shredded cheddar cheese

In large skillet, cook ground beef with chopped onions. When meat is cooked, drain off all grease. Stir in stewed tomatoes with liquid, Worcestershire sauce, salt and pepper. Add 1 cup water. Cook over medium heat until liquid begins to boil. Add rice and stir to blend well. Remove skillet from heat and cover with lid. Meanwhile, wash and core green peppers. Set each pepper in slow cooker. After skillet has set for 10 minutes, uncover, stir and then beginning filling each green pepper cavity. If there is any left over rice mixture, spoon it around the crevices of the green pepper until it is all in the slow cooker. Cover with lid and cook on low for 4-6 hours. Top each stuffed pepper with shredded cheese; as well as each serving of rice and meat.

Chicken Casseroles

CHICKEN MUSHROOM SUPREME ⁰

Prep. Time: about 20 minutes • Serves: 6 • Cost: about 70-cents per serving

1 whole chicken, cut up, skin removed
2¼ cups uncooked instant rice
2 cans cream of mushroom soup
1 can cream of celery soup
2 small cans mushroom pieces, drained
1 medium onion, chopped
1 cup dried bread crumbs
3 tablespoons butter
1 teaspoon salt
¼ teaspoon pepper
3 cups water
2 stalks celery
1 medium onion, left whole
1 teaspoon salt

Remove skin from chicken pieces and place chicken in slow cooker. Add 2 cups water, 2 stalks celery cut in 3-4-inch pieces, 1 whole onion and a teaspoon of salt. Cover with lid and cook on high for 6 hours. Remove meat from slow cooker and empty all vegetables and broth. Let meat cool then pick meat off bones and return small pieces of chicken back to slow cooker. Add cream of mushroom soup, cream of celery soup, 1 cup water, drained mushrooms, uncooked instant rice, medium chopped onion, dried bread crumbs, butter and remaining teaspoon of salt and pepper. Stir to mix well. Cover with lid and cook on high for 3 hours.

Swiss Chicken Casserole

Prep. Time: about 15 minutes • Serves: 6 • Cost: about 69-cents per serving

1 whole chicken, cut into pieces, skin removed
2 cups diced celery
½ lb. Swiss cheese, cut in small cubes or torn in small pieces
about ¾ cup mayonnaise
1 teaspoon salt
¼ teaspoon pepper
¼ cup chopped onions
3 cups water
2 cups uncooked instant rice
1 can (4 oz.) mushrooms, drained
2 teaspoons chopped fresh parsley or 1 teaspoon dried
2 eggs, beaten
2 cans French-styled cut green beans, drained

Coat each piece of chicken with mayonnaise. Discard any remaining mayonnaise. Arrange meat in slow cooker. Add water, celery, onion, and salt. Cover with lid and cook on high for 6 hours. Remove meat from slow cooker and set aside. Combine all remaining ingredients in slow cooker and stir to blend well. Either return meat to slow cooker as is, or remove meat from bones and then return meat to slow cooker. Cover with lid and continue cooking on low for 2-4 hours.

 Plus the Pasta

Anytime a recipe calls for adding pasta, make sure this is done at the end of the cooking time when using a slow cooker. If you add pasta at the beginning of cooking, it will totally disintegrate.

CRUNCHY CHICKEN WITH CASHEWS

Prep. Time: about 20 minutes • Serves: 6 • Cost: about 75-cents per serving

1 whole chicken, cut into pieces, skin removed

3 cups water

1 teaspoon salt

1 onion, chopped

1 cup sliced or diced celery

2 cans French-styled cut green beans, drained

2 packages Uncle Ben® or other named-brand wild rice and chicken blend

3-4 tablespoons butter or margarine

½ cup Miracle Whip® salad dressing or mayonnaise

2 small cans sliced water chestnuts, drained

1 can (4 oz.) mushrooms stems and pieces, drained

1 small can pimentos, diced and drained

1 can cream of celery soup

1 teaspoon salt

½ teaspoon pepper

1 can French fried onion rings, crumbled

1-2 cups cashew pieces

Combine chicken with water, 1 teaspoon salt, onion, and celery in slow cooker. Cover with lid and cook on high for 6 hours. Remove chicken from slow cooker and set aside. Add cream of celery soup and Miracle Whip® and stir to blend well. In separate skillet, melt butter or margarine and brown wild rice mixture lightly. Pour into slow cooker. Add all remaining ingredients and stir to blend well. Remove chicken from bones and return meat to slow cooker. Stir to blend well. Cover with lid and continue cooking on high for 2-4 hours.

CREAMY CHICKEN, BROCCOLI AND RICE CASSEROLE

Prep. Time: about 20 minutes • Serves: 6 • Cost: about 67-cents per serving

1 whole chicken, cut into pieces, skin removed
3 cups water
2 teaspoons salt
2 cups instant rice, uncooked
1 onion, chopped
3 tablespoons butter, melted
¼ cup flour
1½ cups half & half
2 tablespoons chopped parsley
½ teaspoon black pepper
1 pkg. chopped frozen broccoli, thawed
½ cup slivered almonds

Place chicken in slow cooker with water and 1 teaspoon salt. Cover with lid and cook on high for 6 hours. After chicken is cooked, remove chicken and set aside. Pour remaining liquid in measuring cup. In saucepan, melt butter and sauté onion and almonds until onions are transparent. Add flour and stir to make a paste. Add half and half and chicken broth and continue cooking over medium high heat until mixture forms a gravy. Pour mixture into slow cooker. Remove chicken from bones and return meat to slow cooker. Add all remaining ingredients and stir to blend well. Cover with lid and continue cooking on high for 2-4 hours.

CHICKEN BROCCOLI DIVAN

Prep. Time: about 10 minutes • Serves: 6 • Cost: about 69-cents per serving

1 whole chicken, cut up and skin removed
3 cups water
1 teaspoon salt
2 pkgs. frozen broccoli, thawed
2 cans cream of chicken soup
1 teaspoon lemon juice
½ cup mayonnaise
½ teaspoon curry powder
½ cup bread crumbs
1 cup shredded cheddar cheese
3 tablespoons butter, melted

Place chicken in slow cooker with water and 1 teaspoon salt.
Cover with lid and cook on high for 6 hours. Remove chicken from
slow cooker and set aside to cool. Discard or save chicken broth for
another recipe. Place thawed broccoli in bottom of slow cooker. Pick
chicken off bone and tear into bite-sized pieces. Add chicken over
broccoli. In separate bowl, combine cream of chicken soup with
lemon juice, mayonnaise, curry powder and melted butter. Pour
soup mixture over chicken. Top with bread crumbs and cheddar
cheese. Cover with lid and continue cooking on high for 2-4 hours.

Pork Casseroles

L'ORANGE PORK AND RICE

Prep. Time: about 20 minutes • Serves: 6 • Cost: about 71-cents per serving

6 boneless pork chops or pork cutlets
2 cups orange juice
2 cans undiluted chicken and rice soup
1 cup uncooked instant rice
1 teaspoon salt
¼ teaspoon pepper
4 tablespoons butter

In large skillet, melt butter and brown pork in butter on both sides. Remove meat and add uncooked rice. Stir to coat rice well and then remove from heat. Combine all ingredients in slow cooker and lay browned chops on top. Cover with lid and cook on high for 6 hours.

SAUSAGE AND POTATO CASSEROLE

Prep. Time: about 20 minutes • Serves: 6 • Cost: about 52-cents per serving

1 lb. pork sausage
1 can cream of mushroom soup
1 can cream of celery soup
¾ cup milk
1 cup water
1 large onion, chopped
8 medium potatoes, peeled and sliced
2 teaspoons salt
½ teaspoon minced garlic
1 teaspoon black pepper
1½ cups shredded cheddar cheese

Brown sausage in skillet over medium-high heat. Drain meat and crumble into slow cooker. Add all remaining ingredients, except for the cheese. Stir to blend well. Cover with lid and cook on high for 6 hours. Top each serving with cheese.

SAUERKRAUT & SAUSAGE CASSEROLE

Prep. Time: about 20 minutes • Serves: 6 • Cost: about 68-cents per serving

3 large cans sauerkraut, rinsed and drained
2 lbs. Polish sausage, sliced into bite-sized rounds
2 tablespoons caraway seeds
3 tablespoons butter
1 large onion, finely chopped
1 clove of garlic, minced
1 green pepper, diced
1 tablespoon paprika
1 pint sour cream

In skillet on top of stove, melt butter and sauté chopped onion. Add minced garlic and diced green pepper. Cook over medium heat for about 5 minutes, then pour all contents into slow cooker. Drain sauerkraut in a colander and rinse with warm water. Add sauerkraut to slow cooker. Add all remaining ingredients except for the sour cream; stir until well blended. Cover with lid and cook on low for 8 hours. Add sour cream just before ready to serve.

Pork 'n' Beans Casserole

Prep. Time: about 10 minutes • Serves: 6 • Cost: about 49-cents per serving

5 cubed pork or boneless pork loins, cut in strips
2 cans light red kidney beans, undrained
1 can black beans, rinsed
1 can great northern beans, rinsed
1 cup sliced or chopped celery
1 medium sweet onion, chopped
1 cup water
1 cup ketchup
1 can (4 oz.) tomato sauce
½ cup prepared BBQ sauce
½ cup white corn syrup
2 teaspoons salt
½ teaspoon coarse black pepper

Combine water, ketchup, tomato sauce, BBQ sauce, and corn syrup in slow cooker and stir to blend well. Add all remaining ingredients and stir to coat meat and beans. Cover with lid and cook on low for 6 hours.

Cleaning Your Slow Cooker

The easiest way to clean those stubborn rings that are often cooked on to the sides of the slow cooker is to fill the slow cooker with hot tap water and add a tablespoon baking soda. Let this set undisturbed on the counter (away from heat source) until the water becomes lukewarm. Use a plastic scrub pad and lightly scour the ring. By using this method, the baking soda and water will loosen the stain and make cleaning the slow cooker hassle-free.

FARMER JOHN'S PORK CASSEROLE

Prep. Time: about 15 minutes • Serves: 6 • Cost: about 59-cents per serving

1 small (1-3 lbs.) pork shoulder roast
2 cups water
1 teaspoon salt
2 sweet onions, one quartered, one chopped
3 cans French-cut green beans, drained
1 cup sliced celery
¼ cup diced green pepper
1 quart tomato juice
2 cups instant rice, uncooked
1 teaspoon seasoned salt
½ teaspoon coarse black pepper

Set meat in slow cooker and add water. Sprinkle with 1 teaspoon salt. Cover with lid and cook on high for 6 hours. Remove meat from slow cooker and set aside to cool. Discard liquid. Combine all remaining ingredients in slow cooker. Shred cooked pork and return meat pieces to slow cooker. Stir to blend. Cover with lid and continue cooking on high for 2-4 hours.

INDY BACON CASSEROLE

Prep. Time: about 20-25 minutes • Serves: 6 • Cost: about 47-cents per serving

12 slices bacon, fried crisp
4 tablespoons bacon grease
3 cups diced celery
2 cups finely chopped onion
4 cups uncooked instant rice
½ cup canned mushrooms (stems & pieces, okay), drained
1 teaspoon salt
½ teaspoon pepper
2 cans cream of chicken soup
1 cup water
2 cups shredded cheddar cheese (or cheese of your choice)

Combine chicken soup and water in slow cooker. Turn setting on high and cover with lid. In a skillet, fry bacon until crisp. Remove bacon and let drain on paper towel or brown paper. Measure out 4 tablespoons bacon grease and pour off any excess. Return 4 tablespoons bacon grease to hot skillet. Add chopped celery and onion. Fry vegetables until onion turns transparent. Add raw rice and stir often to coat rice with seasoned grease. When all ingredients are heated through, remove skillet from stove and pour contents into slow cooker. Add remaining ingredients and crumbled bacon and mix well. Cover with lid and cook on high for 4 hours.

SHEPHERD'S POT PIE

Prep. Time: about 20 minutes • Servings: 5-6 • Cost: about 64-cents per serving

2 lbs. ground pork or mild bulk sausage
1 small onion, finely chopped
1 can beef vegetable soup
1 teaspoon salt
1 tablespoon sugar
¼ teaspoon black pepper
2 teaspoon oregano
1 can tomato soup
1 can green beans, drained
1 can sliced carrots, drained
1 can refrigerator biscuits 10-count, baked according to directions

In skillet, cook meat with onion. Drain off all grease. Crumble meat and onion into slow cooker. Add both soups, salt, sugar, pepper, oregano and canned vegetables. Stir to mix well. Cover with lid and cook on high for 6 hours or longer. For each serving, tear up two biscuits and spoon pot pie mixture over baked biscuits. Serve immediately.

Vegetable Casseroles

DEEP SOUTH CASSEROLE

Prep. Time: about 20 minutes • Serves 6 • Cost: about 42-cents per serving

1 medium eggplant
1 medium zucchini
1 onion, chopped
¼ cup minced green pepper
1 carrot, diced
2 eggs, beaten
½ cup water
½ cup Parmesan cheese
2 teaspoons salt
½ teaspoon black pepper
2 tablespoons butter

Melt butter in skillet over medium-high heat and cook chopped onion until transparent. Pour butter and onion into slow cooker. Beat eggs and add water, salt, pepper, and cheese. Peel eggplant and zucchini and chop. Put eggplant, zucchini, green pepper, and carrot in slow cooker. Pour egg mixture over vegetables; stir well. Cover slow cooker with lid and cook on high for 4 hours. Reduce heat to low and cook an additional 2 hours.

◖ Lentils and Rice

Prep. Time: about 15 minutes • Serves: 6 • Cost: about 39-cents per serving

1 lb. dried lentils
2 onions, chopped
½ cup butter
2 cups long-grain rice, uncooked
1½ teaspoons ground ginger
1 bay leaf
2 teaspoons salt
½ teaspoon black pepper
Water

The night before cover dried lentils with about 2-inches cold water and let set overnight. Next day, melt butter in skillet over medium-high heat. Sauté onion in butter until transparent. Spoon onions into slow cooker, reserving melted butter and juices. Drain lentils and add lentils to hot butter. Add uncooked rice and cook lentils and rice in hot butter for 5-8 minutes. Pour all into slow cooker with onions. Add remaining ingredients plus 3½ cups water. Cover with lid and cook on high for 4-5 hours, or until lentils and rice are cooked. Adjust seasonings to your desired taste.

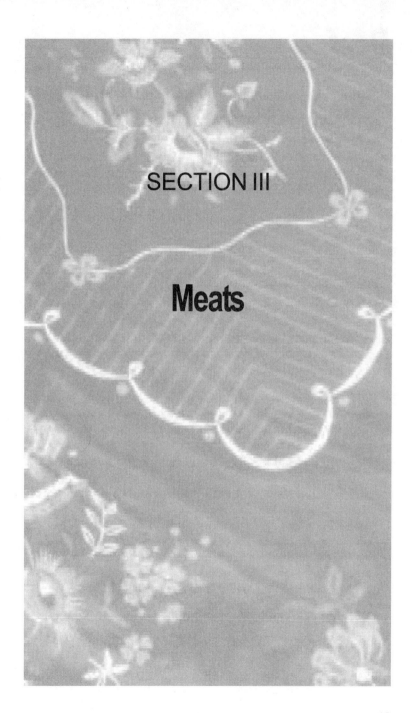

SECTION III

Meats

Beef

BARBECUED SPARERIBS

Prep. Time: 5 minutes • Serves: 6 • Cost: about 39-cents per serving

Spareribs, cut into pieces
BBQ sauce of your choice
2 onions, sliced and separated into rings
2 cups water
1 teaspoon salt

Combine all ingredients in large slow cooker. Cover with lid and cook on high for 10-12 hours.

 Cooking Unplugged

Slow cookers should be unplugged when not in use. Don't learn this rule the hard way like I had to do. Since my slow cookers are stored on my kitchen island counter-top, the kids will occasionally lay their papers on top of the slow cooker. One day while I had the crocks in the sink waiting to be washed, my daughter set a half-sheet paper up on the slow cooker unit. She was too small to realize the crock was not in the shell. And I had forgotten to turn off the slow cooker which was on the low setting. It wasn't long before we started smelling something burning. Fortunately I found the source before a full-fledged fire broke out. This could have been completely avoided had I remembered to unplug the slow cooker when I was finished cooking. I've also heard that appliances that are plugged in, even if they are turned off, still consume electricity.

Beef & Olives

Prep. Time: about 10 minutes • Serves: 6 • Cost: about 69-cents per serving

3 - 4 lbs. chuck roast, trimmed of visible excess fat
1 onion, sliced
1 cup salad olives with juice
1 teaspoon salt
½ teaspoon pepper
2 tablespoons Worcestershire sauce

Place meat in slow cooker. Add Worcestershire sauce to olive juice and stir to blend. Pour olives and juice over meat. Cover with sliced onions. Sprinkle salt and pepper over all. Cover with lid and cook on high for 6-8 hours.

Sloppy Joes

Prep. Time: about 15 minutes • Serves: 6 • Cost: about 43-cents per serving

2 lbs. lean ground beef or turkey
1 large onion, finely chopped
1 green pepper, finely chopped
1 tablespoon Worcestershire Sauce
1 cup ketchup
1 small can tomato paste
¼ cup brown sugar, heaping
¼ cup white corn syrup
1 teaspoon garlic powder
1 teaspoon salt
¼ teaspoon coarse black pepper

In large soup pan, cover meat with water and bring to a boil. Cook meat until done. Drain well. Crumble cooked ground meat in slow cooker along with all remaining ingredients. Stir to blend well. Cover with lid and let cook on low for 4-6 hours.

Garlic & Thyme Beef Steak

Prep. Time: about 15 minutes • Serves: 6 • Cost: about 47-cents per serving

2 - 3 lbs. lean round steak, cut into serving portions
¼ cup flour
1 teaspoon salt
1/8 teaspoon pepper
1 teaspoon garlic powder
2 teaspoons ground thyme
1 onion, sliced
2 cups water, boiling
3 beef bouillon cubes
1 packet brown gravy mix
1 cup fresh mushroom slices
¼ cup light sour cream (may use fat free)

In a baggie, combine flour with salt, pepper, garlic powder and thyme. Taking one piece at a time, drop meat in baggie and shake to evenly coat. Place floured and seasoned meat in slow cooker. Slice onion and arrange over meat. Add sliced mushrooms. In boiling water, dissolve 3 beef bouillon cubes and brown gravy mix. Pour over meat. Cover with lid and cook on high for 6 hours. Remove meat from slow cooker. Add sour cream to remaining juices; stir to blend well. Pour over meat and serve.

SEASONED BEEF ROAST WITH ZIP

Prep. Time: about 5 minutes • Servings: 6+ • Cost: about 48-cents per serving

3-4 lbs. chuck beef roast
1 can cream of mushroom soup
1 envelope onion soup mix
2 tablespoons Tabasco sauce

Set meat in slow cooker. In separate container, combine mushroom soup with dry soup and Tabasco sauce. Mix well. Pour over meat. Cover with lid and cook on high for 7-9 hours.

CHUCK ROAST WITH MUSHROOMS

Prep. Time: about 10 minutes • Serves: 6+ • Cost: about 50-cents per serving

3-4 lb. chuck roast
1 pkg. dry onion soup mix
1 lb. fresh mushrooms, left whole
2 cups water
2 packets brown gravy mix

Dissolve soup and gravy mixes in water. Place meat in slow cooker. Add mushrooms. Pour onion soup mixture over all. Cover with lid and cook on high for 7-9 hours.

BEEF SHOULDER

Prep. Time: about 10 minutes • Serves: 6+ • Cost: about 53-cents per serving

3-4 lbs. beef shoulder arm
2 teaspoons salt
¼ teaspoon pepper
1 large onion, sliced
1 cup water
1 can cream of mushroom soup
1 pint Penny's Garden Medley Sauce (see Supplemental Chapter,
    page 82)

In slow cooker, combine soup with garden medley sauce and
water. Add salt and pepper. Mix well. Add meat to slow cooker.
Spoon soup mixture over meat. Arrange slices of onion over meat.
Cover with lid and cook on high for 8 hours.

🍲 TANGY BEEF ROAST

*Prep. Time: about 10 minutes • Serves: 6 * Cost: about 56-cents per serving*

3-4 lb. chuck roast
2 onions, chopped
1 bay leaf
1 teaspoon salt
1 cup water
3 tablespoons brown sugar
¼ cup ketchup
¼ cup raisins
1 tablespoon cider vinegar

Place meat in slow cooker after trimming off any visible fat. Cover meat with chopped onions. Add bay leaf. In separate bowl, combine water with salt, brown sugar, ketchup, raisins and cider vinegar. Stir to blend well. Pour over meat. Cover with lid and cook on high 7-9 hours.

🍲 EASY CHUCK ROAST

Prep. Time: less than 5 minutes • Serves: 6 • Cost: about 43-cents per serving

2-3 lbs. chuck roast
2 beef bouillon cubes
1 teaspoon salt
¼ teaspoon pepper

Place roast in slow cooker. Do not add any water or other liquid. Place bouillon cubes on top of roast (as if they were eyes staring back at you). Sprinkle with salt and pepper. Cover with lid and cook on high for 3 hours. Reduce heat setting to low and continue cooking for 6-7 hours more. Slice and serve.

Chicken

◊ HAWAIIAN CHICKEN

Prep. Time: about 15 minutes • Serves: 6 • Cost: about 54-cents per serving

1 whole chicken, cut into pieces, skin removed
¼ cup soy sauce
1 tablespoon dried minced onion
¼ teaspoon ground ginger
1 can (1 lb. 4 oz) pineapple chunks, reserve juice
2 tablespoons lemon juice

Remove skin from chicken pieces. Put chicken in slow cooker. In a separate container, combine soy sauce, minced onion, ground ginger, lemon juice and the juice drained from the can of pineapple. Stir or shake to blend well. Drizzle seasoning sauce over chicken, using all of the sauce. Cover with lid and cook on high for 6 hours. Check chicken for doneness. Depending upon weight of chicken, you may need to let this cook for an additional 1-2 hours on high. When ready to serve, remove chicken from slow cooker and arrange on a serving platter. Pour pineapple chunks into slow cooker and stir to mix with juices. Spoon warmed pineapple chunks and sauce over chicken.

Scalloped Chicken

Prep. Time: about 20-25 minutes • Serves: 6 • Cost: about 52-cents per serving

1 whole chicken, cut into pieces
3 cups water
¼ green pepper, chopped
1 jar pimento, drained and chopped
12 hard-cooked eggs, chopped
2 cans evaporated milk
2 cups sliced fresh mushrooms
¼ stick butter or margarine
1 small onion, chopped
3 cups chicken broth, reserved from cooking chicken
¼ cup flour
1 teaspoon salt, add more or less to taste
¼ teaspoon black pepper

Place chicken in slow cooker. Add 3 cups water. Cover with lid and cook on high for 5 hours. Remove meat and set aside to cool. Strain broth, reserving 3 cups clear broth. In large skillet, melt butter and saute chopped onion, green pepper and pimento until onion turns transparent. Add flour and stir until pasty. Stir in strained chicken broth and cook over medium heat until mixture begins to thicken. Let simmer while you pick chicken off the bones and tear into bite-sized pieces. Put cooked chicken, sliced mushrooms and the thickened gravy into slow cooker. Add remaining ingredients. Cover with lid and cook on low for 3 hours.

Chicken Thermidor

Prep. Time: about 20 minutes • Serves: 6 • Cost: about 65-cents per serving

1 whole chicken, cut up, skin removed
4 cups water
2 stalks celery
1 large onion, quartered
1 cup diced celery
1 can (5 oz) water chestnuts, drained and sliced
¼ cup toasted sliced almonds
2 tablespoons chopped green pepper
1 tablespoon grated onion
2 tablespoons chopped pimento
2 tablespoons white wine
1 tablespoon lemon juice
¼ teaspoon salt
¼ cup milk
1 can cream of chicken soup
2 slices bread, cubed
1 cup shredded Cheddar cheese

Arrange chicken in slow cooker. Add stalks of celery and quartered onion. Pour 3 cups water over meat and cover with lid. Cook
on high for 6 hours. Remove chicken and discard vegetables.
Strain broth and save for use in another recipe. Add 1 cup water
to slow cooker. Add diced celery, sliced chestnuts, sliced almonds, chopped green peppers, grated onion, and chopped
pimento. Add white wine, lemon juice, salt, milk, soup and cubed
bread. Pick chicken off bone and tear into bite-sized pieces. Add
meat to slow cooker. Stir to blend well. Cover with lid and cook on
low for 3 hours. Add cheese the last hour of cooking.

BBQ Chicken

Prep. Time: about 15 minutes • Serves: 6 • Cost: about 49-cents per serving

1 whole chicken, cut up, skin removed
¼ cup ketchup
3 tablespoons vinegar
¼ cup water
3 tablespoons brown sugar
1 tablespoon prepared mustard
1 teaspoon salt
1 teaspoon seasoned salt
2 tablespoons Worcestershire sauce
¼ teaspoon black pepper
2 tablespoons dried minced onions
2 cups water
2 stalks celery
1 whole onion

Arrange chicken pieces in slow cooker. Pour in 2 cups water. Add 2 stalks of celery and 1 whole onion. Cover with lid and cook on high for 6 hours. Remove onion and celery and discard. Remove chicken from slow cooker and set aside. Drain off liquid. In a separate container, combine all the remaining ingredients and stir to blend well. Return chicken to slow cooker. Pour BBQ sauce over chicken. Cover with lid and cook on low for 2-3 hours before serving.

Paprika Chicken Breasts

Prep. Time: about 15 minutes • Serves: 6 • Cost: about 52-cents per serving

5-6 chicken breasts, boneless and skinless
2 medium yellow onions, chopped
1/8 teaspoon cayenne pepper
¼ stick butter
2 tablespoons paprika
2 tablespoons flour
1 teaspoon salt
2 cups water
1 cup sour cream (may use light or fat free)

Cut chicken breasts into fourths. Turn slow cooker on high. Melt butter in slow cooker. Add pepper, paprika, flour and salt; stir to blend well. Pour in water and stir to blend well. Add chicken and chopped onions. Cover with lid and cook on high for 6 hours. Add sour cream just before serving. This goes good with cooked rice or noodles.

⊛ "Baked" Chicken and Mushrooms

Prep. Time: about 15 minutes • Serves: 6 • Cost: about 63-cents per serving

5 chicken breasts, skin removed
1 can mushrooms stems & pieces (small or large)
1 can cream of mushroom soup
1 can cream of chicken soup
1 soup can milk
1 envelope dry onion soup mix

Remove skin from chicken breasts and split breasts in half. Combine soups with milk in slow cooker. Stir in dry onion soup mix and drained mushrooms. Add chicken, coating each piece with the soup mixture. Cover with lid. Cook on high for 6 hours or until chicken meat forks easily away from bone and juices run clear.

⊛ Salsafied Chicken

Prep. Time: about 15 minutes • Serves: 6 • Cost: about 53-cents per serving

5 whole chicken breasts, skinned and split
¼ cup Regular Miracle Whip® (don't use Fat Free or Light)
1 bottle chunky salsa (your choice: mild, medium, hot)
1 teaspoon chili powder
¼ teaspoon ground cumin
1 teaspoon salt
1 teaspoon celery flakes
1 teaspoon basil
1 teaspoon parsley flakes

Remove skin from chicken breasts and split each in half. Rub Miracle Whip® over each chicken breast. In a separate container, combine chili powder, cumin, salt, celery flakes, basil and parsley flakes. Pat on to covered chicken breasts. Arrange chicken in slow cooker. Pour salsa over chicken. Cover with lid and cook on high for 6 hours or longer.

◦ THE KING'S CHICKEN

Prep. Time: about 15 minutes • Serves: 6 • Cost: about 46-cents per serving

5 whole chicken breasts, skin removed, split
¼ cup fresh parsley, chopped
1 teaspoon salt
¼ teaspoon pepper
¼ cup melted butter
1 clove garlic, peeled

Remove skin from each piece of chicken. Split each breast in half. Rinse chicken with warm water and arrange in slow cooker. In separate container, melt butter and add salt and pepper. Stir to blend well and drizzle over chicken pieces. Add garlic clove to slow cooker. Sprinkle fresh parsley over chicken pieces. Cover with lid and cook on high for 6 - 7 hours. Remove garlic before serving.

PENNY'S CREAMY CHICKEN & MUSHROOMS

Prep. Time: about 15 minutes • Serves: 6 • Cost: about 67-cents per serving

5 whole chicken breasts
1 can cream of mushroom soup
1 can cream of chicken soup
1 can cream of celery soup
1 soup can water
1 teaspoon rosemary
1 teaspoon paprika
1 teaspoon salt
¼ teaspoon black pepper
2 cups fresh mushroom slices
1 teaspoon parsley
1 cup sour cream

Remove skin from chicken breasts and split each in half. Rinse in warm water and arrange in slow cooker. In separate container, combine soups with water, rosemary, parsley, salt and pepper. Stir to blend well and pour over chicken in slow cooker. Sprinkle paprika over chicken. Cover with lid and cook on high for 6 - 7 hours.

Guatemalan Chicken

Prep. Time: about 25 minutes Serves: 6 Cost: about 64-cents per serving

1 whole fryer chicken, cut up in pieces
¼ cup white vinegar
1 cup honey
1 cup ketchup
¼ cup oil
¼ cup flour
¼ cup yellow corn meal
1 teaspoon salt
¼ teaspoon black pepper

Cut up chicken and wash each piece. In a shallow dish or a plastic bag, combine flour, corn meal, salt and pepper. Dip each piece of chicken into flour mixture, coating the entire piece evenly. In large skillet, heat oil over medium high heat. Add coated chicken pieces. Cook until lightly browned on all sides. Remove chicken from skillet and place in slow cooker. In separate bowl combine vinegar with honey and ketchup. Stir to blend well and then pour sauce over chicken pieces, being sure to cover all pieces of chicken. Cover with lid and cook on high for 5 hours.

ROCK CORNISH GAME HENS

Prep. Time: about 10 minutes • Serves: 6+ • Cost: about 58-cents per serving

4 Rock Cornish Game Hens, thawed
2 teaspoons salt
¾ teaspoon black pepper
1 stick butter, melted
1 teaspoon paprika
1 large jar currant jelly

Place hens in slow cooker. Drizzle melted butter over hens. Sprinkle with salt, pepper and paprika. Cover with lid and cook on high for 4 hours. Spoon currant jelly over each hen, letting the jelly melt and glaze each hen. Return lid over slow cooker after coating hens with jelly. Continue cooking on high for a total of 6-7 hours.

Pork

◦ Penny's Pork Chops

Prep. Time: about 10 minutes • Serves: 6+ • Cost: about 59-cents per serving

6-8 pork chops, trimmed of fat
1 teaspoon salt
¼ teaspoon pepper
1 can cream of chicken soup
1 can cream of celery soup
¼ teaspoon dry mustard
¼ teaspoon garlic powder
1 onion, chopped
1 cup celery, diced

Combine all ingredients in slow cooker except meat. Stir to blend well. Dip each chop into slow cooker mixture and then layer chops in center. Cover with lid and cook on low for 6-8 hours.

◦ Spanish Pork Chops

Prep. Time: about 5 minutes • Serves: 6 • Cost: about 54-cents per serving

6 pork chops, trimmed of fat
1 onion, chopped
2 cups canned stewed tomatoes with juice
1 teaspoon salt
¼ teaspoon black pepper
2¼ cups uncooked rice
4 cups water

Combine all ingredients in slow cooker. Cover with lid and cook on low for 8 hours. Adjust seasonings according to taste.

SPICY PORK CHOPS

Prep. Time: about 10 minutes • Serves: 6 • Cost: about 53-cents per serving

6 pork chops, trimmed of fat
1 onion, chopped
2 cans cream of mushroom soup
¼ teaspoon cayenne or red pepper
1 cup stewed tomatoes with juice
1 cup water
2 stalks celery, diced
1 teaspoon salt
¼ teaspoon black pepper

Combine all ingredients in slow cooker. Cover with lid and cook on low for 8 hours. Rice may be added to slow cooker and cooked after meat is removed. Taste and adjust seasonings.

❖ BBQ RIBS

Prep. Time: about 35 minutes • Serves: 6+ • Cost: about 39-cents per serving

4-6 lbs. country ribs, lean
2 large onions
1 bottle BBQ sauce
Water
Salt

Cover ribs with water in a large soup pan. Add ¼ teaspoon salt.
Bring to a boil and let cook for about 30 minutes. Remove ribs
from soup pan and place them in slow cooker. Pour prepared
BBQ sauce over ribs. Add slices of onion. Sprinkle with salt.
Cover with lid and cook on low for 7-9 hours.

❖ PORK SHANK WITH SAUERKRAUT

Prep. Time: about 10 minutes • Serves: 6+ • Cost: about 43-cents per serving

Pork shank, cut into pieces small enough to fit in slow cooker
2 cans sauerkraut, drained
2 cups tomato juice
1¼ cups rice
Water

Arrange pork in slow cooker. Cover with water and lid and cook on
high for 5 hours. Drain off all liquid. Add all remaining ingredients.
Cover with lid and continue cooking on low for 2-3 hours.

Honey Glazed Ham

Prep. Time: about 10 minutes • Serves: 6+ • Cost: about 49-cents per serving

1 canned ham, rinsed and patted dry whole cloves
¼ cup orange juice
¼ cup brown sugar
1 tablespoon prepared mustard
¼ cup honey
2 oranges, sliced, seeds removed

Score the top of the ham and insert cloves in the center of orange slices, securing each slice to the top of the ham. Set ham in slow cooker. In separate bowl, combine all ingredients and mix well. Pour over ham. Cover with lid and cook on low for 7-9 hours.

☜ PERFECT PORK CHOPS

Prep. Time: about 10 minutes • Serves: 6+ • Cost: about 48-cents per serving

6-8 pork chops, trimmed of fat
2 cups Coca-Cola®, regular not diet
1 can pineapple chunks
1 cup ketchup

Arrange chops in slow cooker. Add pineapple chunks. In separate bowl, combine remaining pineapple juice with Coca-Cola® and ketchup. Pour over chops. Cover with lid and cook on low for 7 hours.

◦ SWEET & TANGY CHOPS

Prep. Time: about 10 minutes • Serves: 6 • Cost: about 65-cents per serving

6 pork chops, trimmed of fat
2 fresh lemons, sliced
1 large onion, sliced
¼ cup ketchup mixed with ¼ cup water
Brown sugar

Lay a pork chop in the bottom of the slow cooker. Sprinkle brown sugar over meat. Lay a thin slice of onion on chop. Add a slice of lemon over the onion. Lay another pork chop in slow cooker. Repeat. Pour watered-down ketchup over all. Cover with lid and cook on low for 7 hours.

PORK ROAST WITH SWEET POTATOES

Prep. Time: about 15 minutes •   Serves: 6+ • Cost: about 63-cents per serving

3-4 lbs. pork roast, fat trimmed
3-4 sweet potatoes or yams, peeled, cut in thick 2-inch slices
¼ cup apricot preserves
¼ cup crushed pineapple, drained
¼ cup concentrated orange juice from a frozen concentrate
1 tablespoon soy sauce
¼ teaspoon ground ginger
¼ teaspoon pepper

Slice sweet potatoes and place them in the bottom of the slow
cooker. Set pork roast on top of potato slices. In separate bowl,
combine remaining ingredients and stir to blend well. Pour
mixture over meat and potatoes. Cover with lid and cook on high
for 6 hours or 12 hours on low.

SIMPLE ROAST PORK

Prep. Time: about 10 minutes • Serves: 6+ • Cost: about 49-cents per serving

3-5 lbs. pork roast or loin of pork
¼ teaspoon thyme
1 teaspoon salt
¼ teaspoon black pepper
¼ cup water

Place meat in slow cooker. Add water. Sprinkle thyme, salt and pepper over meat. Cover with lid and cook on high for 6 hours. Check meat for tenderness. Reduce heat and continue cooking for 2-3 hours if meat is not fork-tender after the initial 6 hours of cooking time.

Multi-Use Slow Cookers

Did you know you can use your removable slow cooker in the oven, too? You can! I've done this numerous times with success. What I've found though is the slow cooker forms a "vapor lock" with the lid as it heats and cooks. You'll still get "moist and tender" results since you're using a slow cooker, but it will take less time in the oven since you're really baking. I've done this to "hurry along" slow cooker dishes, too. Just be careful when removing the lid after its been in the oven. It will be "locked" to the slow cooker and it will be holding in lots of hot steam.

Wild or Game

The following recipes do not take into account any cost considerations for the meat. The estimate for these recipes is based on the assumption the meat is either caught by, or, given to you.

SEASONED VENISON ROAST

Prep. Time: about 15 minutes • Serves: 6+ • Cost: about 32-cents per serving

1 (3-4 lbs.) venison roast
1 can (8 oz.) tomato sauce
1 bay leaf
1 teaspoon oregano
1 teaspoon basil
1 teaspoon salt
¼ teaspoon black pepper
1 tablespoon Worcestershire sauce

Place venison roast in slow cooker. Pour tomato sauce over meat. Sprinkle seasonings over meat. Add bay leaf to slow cooker. Cover with lid and cook on high for 8 hours.

Venison and Mushroom Bake

Prep. Time: about 20 minutes • Serves: 6+ • Cost: about 42-cents per serving

2-4 lbs. venison, cut into bite-sized pieces
6-9 potatoes, peeled and cubed
1 onion, chopped
¼ green pepper, chopped
2 cups sliced fresh mushrooms
2 packets brown gravy mix prepared according to
   package directions
1 stalk celery, sliced
1 teaspoon salt
¼ teaspoon black pepper

Cut meat into bite-sized pieces. Combine meat with chopped potatoes, onion, green pepper, celery and mushrooms in slow cooker. Stir to blend well. Pour prepared brown gravy over contents in slow cooker. Sprinkle with salt and pepper. Cover with lid and cook on high for 6-7 hours.

Saucy Venison

Prep. Time: about 10 minutes • Serves: 6+ • Cost: about 28-cents per serving

3-4 lbs. venison, cut into serving pieces
2 teaspoons salt
¼ teaspoon pepper
¼ teaspoon paprika
¾ cup white vinegar
1 cup brown sugar
1 cup water
2 tablespoons cornstarch dissolved in ¼ cup water

Combine all ingredients in slow cooker, except cornstarch water. Cover with lid and cook on low for 6 hours. Add cornstarch water to the sauce after the meat is removed. Increase heat to high and cook for 15 minutes to slightly thicken. Serve with cooked rice or mashed potatoes.

TANGY VENISON BBQ

Prep. Time: about 15-20 minutes • Serves: 6+ • Cost: about 39-cents per serving

3-4 lbs. venison stew meat
2 onions, chopped
3-4 cloves garlic, chopped
1 cup red wine vinegar
¼ cup Worcestershire sauce
2 teaspoons seasoning salt
1 lb. bacon, fried crisp, drained
2 cups ketchup
¼ cup molasses
¼ cup brown sugar

Combine venison stew meat with chopped onions, garlic, red wine vinegar, Worcestershire sauce, salt, ketchup, molasses and brown sugar. Cover with lid and cook on high for 4 hours. In skillet, fry bacon until crisp and drain off grease. Crumble bacon in slow cooker. Cover with lid and continue cooking for 8 to 12 hours on the low setting.

HERBED VENISON STEAK

Prep. Time: about 15 minutes • Serves: 6+ • Cost: about 37-cents per serving

6-8 pieces boneless venison steak
2 onions, finely chopped
1 tablespoon brown sugar
1 teaspoon salt
1 teaspoon seasoned salt
¼ teaspoon pepper
pinch of cayenne
1 teaspoon oregano
¼ teaspoon thyme
1 teaspoon sage
1 teaspoon basil
1 tablespoon chopped capers
¼ cup ketchup
¼ cup Worcestershire sauce
¼ cup white vinegar

Place a single layer of meat in slow cooker. Cover with chopped onions. Combine salt, seasoned salt, pepper, cayenne, oregano, thyme, sage, and basil in baggie; shake to mix well. Sprinkle seasoning mixture over onions. Add another layer of meat and cover with chopped onions. Sprinkle seasoning mixture over onions; repeat until all meat and onions are in slow cooker. In separate container, combine chopped capers with ketchup, Worcestershire sauce, and vinegar. Mix well and pour over meat. Cover with lid and cook on high for 7-8 hours.

"Brew" Rabbit

Prep. Time: about 20 minutes • Serves: 6+ • Cost: about 44-cents per serving

2-3 dressed rabbits, cut into pieces
2 tablespoons oil
1 large onion, chopped
1 can warm beer
¼ cup prepared chili sauce
¼ cup brown sugar
2 teaspoons minced garlic
1¼ teaspoons salt

Clean dressed rabbits and cut into pieces. Arrange meat in slow cooker. Drizzle oil over meat and sprinkle with brown sugar and salt. Add chopped onion over rabbit and pour chili sauce over meat. Pour warm beer down side of slow cooker, being careful not to pour directly over rabbit (so seasonings stay on). Add minced garlic to slow cooker. Cover with lid and cook on low for 6-8 hours or until tender.

WILD RABBIT

Prep. Time: about 20 minutes • Serves: 6 • Cost: about 48-cents per serving

2-3 wild rabbits, dressed and cut up
1¼ cups olive or salad oil
2 cloves garlic
1¼ cups flour
1 tablespoon dry mustard
1 teaspoon curry powder
1 teaspoon powdered thyme
2 teaspoons salt
¼ teaspoon pepper
1 cup chicken broth

Rub rabbit pieces with oil and let set overnight in the refrigerator. Cut garlic cloves and rub directly over greased rabbit. In large plastic bag, combine flour, dry mustard, curry powder, powdered thyme, salt and pepper and mix well. Add pieces of meat one at a time and shake until well coated. Fry to a golden brown in a large skillet. Transfer browned rabbit to slow cooker. Add chicken broth. Cover with lid and cook on low for 6 hours.

SECTION IV

Supplemental Recipes

This chapter is where you'll find all sauces and sides. Please note for the sauces, these recipes produce a batch that can be canned or frozen and used over time in numerous recipes. If there's an exception, I've made a note with the individual recipe(s).

Also, guess-timating the cost per serving for sauces is almost impossible for me since I use fresh garden produce I've raised myself. Therefore, there will not be a cost per serving estimate for sauces.

Sauces

Penny's Garden Medley Sauce

Prep. Time: about 30 minutes • Yield: about 6 pints

15 to 20 fresh tomatoes, blemish free
2-3 large onions
3 stalks of celery
1 green pepper, seeds & core removed
1 tablespoon minced garlic
2 teaspoons salt
¾ teaspoon black pepper
1 teaspoon crushed oregano or cilantro
2-3 cups water
2-4 large carrots—optional
1-2 summer squash and/or zucchini—optional (these add nutritional
    value but do not affect the taste)

Prepare fresh tomatoes, then quarter the tomatoes and place in
slow cooker, seeds and all.

Add all the remaining ingredients until slow cooker is full. Cook
all day on high or for at least 6 hours. Turn slow cooker off and let
contents cool. Scoop out cooked vegetables 1-2 cups at a time and
put them in a blender. Puree. Pour pureed sauce in separate bowl or
pan. Continue blending the vegetables until only sauce remains.

Fill freezer containers or canning jars and process. Keep this
sauce in your pantry for use in other recipes.

Bulgarian Spaghetti Sauce

Prep. Time: about 15 minutes • Yield: about 3 cups

1 quart of canned tomatoes or 4 cups of fresh tomatoes, peeled and
    cored
1 large can (12 oz.) tomato paste
1 large onion, diced
1 teaspoon minced garlic
3 tablespoons oil—optional
1 cup water
1½ teaspoon salt
½ teaspoon pepper
1½ teaspoon oregano
1-2 whole dried bay leaves

Add all ingredients to slow cooker and cook on low for over 6
hours or on high for up to 4 hours. Remove bay leaves before
serving. NOTE: I use one batch of this recipe when making
spaghetti for my family of 5. We like our spaghetti rather saucy
and this is just the right amount. For smaller families, I recom-
mend dividing the sauce and only using half per meal.

SAUSAGE, MUSHROOMS & ZUCCHINI SPAGHETTI SAUCE

Prep. Time: about 15 minutes • Yield: about 3 cups

1 lb. Italian sausage

2 medium onions, finely chopped

1 lb. fresh mushrooms, cut in bits and pieces or left in whole slices

1 small zucchini, grated

1 small green pepper, diced

3 large tomatoes, skins removed, diced

2 cans (8 oz.) tomato sauce

1 teaspoon salt

½ teaspoon pepper

2 teaspoons oregano

2 teaspoons Italian seasoning

1 teaspoon basil

Combine all ingredients in slow cooker. Stir to blend well. Cover with lid and cook on low for 7 hours. Serve over hot pasta. NOTE: This recipe makes enough spaghetti sauce for one large meal.

GREEK SPAGHETTI SAUCE

Prep. Time: about 15 minutes • Yield: between 2-3 cups

1 lb. lean ground beef
2 tablespoons olive oil
1 large clove garlic, minced
½ cup red wine or sherry
1 (1 lb.) can stewed tomatoes with juice
1 (6 oz.) can tomato paste
2-inch stick of cinnamon, broken in pieces
8-10 whole cloves
1 teaspoon salt
½ teaspoon pepper

Brown meat and minced garlic in olive oil and then drain on a
paper towel or brown paper when meat is fully cooked through.
Tie spices up in a bag of cheesecloth. Combine all ingredients in
slow cooker and add 1 tomato-paste-can of water. Cover with lid
and cook on low for 5 hours. For a thicker sauce cook on high for
8 hours, removing the lid after the first 2-3 hours of cooking time.
Serve over cooked pasta. NOTE: This recipe produces enough for
one large meal.

HOMEMADE BBQ SAUCE FOR RIBS OR CHOPS

Prep. Time: about 5 minutes • Yield: between 2-3 cups

½ cup brown sugar
2 teaspoons salt
½ teaspoon garlic powder
2 cups ketchup
1 large onion, diced
1 teaspoon paprika
½ teaspoon dry mustard
3 tablespoons Worcestershire sauce™
¼ cup cider vinegar
½ teaspoon black pepper
1 teaspoon chili powder

Combine all ingredients in slow cooker. Cover with lid and cook on low for 6 hours. Sauce may be stored in refrigerator for up to two weeks.

HOMEMADE CHILI SAUCE

Prep. Time: about 15 minutes • Yield: between 4-5 pints

1 quart of tomato juice
1 quart of canned tomatoes, diced or pureed
1 whole onion, peeled and quartered
2 tablespoons of chili powder (add more or less to taste)
1 tablespoon salt (add or subtract according to taste)
1 tablespoon Steak Sauce
1 seeded jalapeno pepper or 2 seeded hot banana
    peppers

Combine all ingredients in slow cooker. Stir to blend well. Cover with lid and cook on low for 6 hours. Taste and adjust seasonings. Freeze or can for later use.

Sides

Here are recipes for side dishes you can prepare to complete your meal.

CALICO BEANS

Prep. Time: about 15 minutes • Servings: 6 • Cost: about 19-cents per serving

½ cup ketchup
1 teaspoon salt
¾ cup brown sugar, firmly packed
1½ teaspoons dry mustard
8 slices bacon
½ cup white corn syrup
1 can red kidney beans
1 can pork 'n' beans
1 can Great Northern beans
½ to 1 lb. lean ground beef, pork, or turkey
1 onion, chopped

In skillet, cook ground meat with onion until browned. Drain off all grease. Pour meat and onion into slow cooker. Chop slices of raw bacon into little pieces and add to slow cooker. Add beans with their liquids and all remaining ingredients. Stir well to blend ingredients. Cover slow cooker with lid and turn on low to cook 6 hours.

SMOKED BAKED BEANS

Prep. Time: about 15 minutes • Serves: 6 • Cost: about 21 cents per serving

8 slices bacon, cut in pieces
3 (16 oz.) cans pork 'n' beans
1 cup brown sugar, firmly packed
1 tablespoon dried minced onion
1 tablespoon chili powder
2 teaspoons dry mustard
1 teaspoon liquid smoke
1 cup prepared BBQ sauce
½ cup ketchup
¼ cup molasses or dark corn syrup

Combine all ingredients in slow cooker. Stir to blend well. Cover with lid and cook on low for 6 hours. Stir well before serving.

FRESH GREEN BEANS

Prep. Time: about 20 minutes • Serves: 6 • Cost: about 23-cents per serving

Wash and snap 2 lbs. fresh green beans
2 onions, chopped
1 smoked ham hock
2 cups water
2 teaspoons salt
new red potatoes, scrubbed clean, optional

Set smoked ham hock in center of slow cooker. Add snapped green beans around hock. Spread chopped onions on top of green beans. Add water and salt, and new red potatoes if desired. Cover with lid and cook on low for 8-9 hours.

French Onion Green Beans

Prep. Time: about 5 minutes • Serves: 6+ • Cost: about .27-cents per serving

2 quarts green beans, drained
2 cans cream of mushroom soup
1 cup milk
5 strips bacon, cut in thin pieces
1 onion, finely chopped
1 can (2.8 oz) French fried onions

Combine all ingredients except for the French fried onions. Stir to blend well. Cover with lid and cook on low for 5 hours. Top with the French fried onions before serving.

Country Cabbage

Prep. Time: about 20 minutes • Serves: 6 • Cost: about 17-cents per serving

1 head cabbage, chopped (discard core)
1 teaspoon salt
1/8 teaspoon black pepper
1 cup water
1 carrot, grated

Combine all the above ingredients and put in slow cooker. Cover with lid and cook on high for 4 hours. Add sauce from next page.

White Sauce for Country Cabbage

3 tablespoons butter
3 tablespoons flour
1 teaspoon salt
¼ teaspoon black pepper
2 cups milk

In medium skillet, melt butter over low heat. Add flour, salt and pepper and stir to make a paste. Increase heat to medium and gradually stir in milk. Stir constantly to dissolve paste in milk. Continue to cook over medium heat, stirring constantly until sauce thickens into a gravy consistency. When sauce is desired consistency, remove from heat and pour over cabbage in slow cooker. Turn heat setting to low and let cook for 1 more hour before serving. This may cook longer on the low setting if you desire.

Carrots 'n' Cream

Prep. Time: about 10 minutes • Serves: 6+ • Cost: about 41-cents per serving

8 large carrots, sliced
2 pkgs. (8 oz) cream cheese
2 cans cream of celery soup
salt and pepper to taste

Combine all ingredients in slow cooker. Stir to blend well. Cover with lid and cook on high for 6 hours. Stir and serve.

Scalloped Corn

Prep. Time: about 5 minutes • Serves: 6 • Cost: about 22-cents per serving

2 cans cream-style corn
1 can sweet whole kernal corn, drained
6 large eggs
2 cups milk
1 teaspoon salt
¼ teaspoon pepper
½ teaspoon seasoned salt
2 cups crushed saltine crackers

Combine all ingredients in slow cooker. Cover with lid and cook on low for 6 hours.

Italian Vegetable Blend

Prep. Time: about 10 minutes • Serves: 6 • Cost: about 29-cents per serving

1 medium zucchini, cubed
2 cans French style green beans, drained
1 onion, chopped
1 can (16 oz.) stewed tomatoes
2 teaspoons salt
½ teaspoon black pepper
1 teaspoon oregano
1 teaspoon basil
¼ cup Parmesan cheese

Combine all ingredients in slow cooker. Stir to blend well. Cover with lid and cook on low for 4-6 hours.

CHEESY SHREDDED POTATOES

Prep. Time: about 15 minutes • Serves: 6+ • Cost: about 53-cents per serving

2 lb. frozen shredded hash browns, thawed, or fresh potatoes,
    shredded
1 can cream of chicken soup
1 lb. processed American cheese, cubed
1 can (4 oz.) mushrooms, drained—optional
1 pint sour cream (may use fat free or plain yogurt)
½ stick butter or margarine, melted
1 onion, chopped finely
Parsley flakes

Add thawed hash browns to slow cooker, along with all other
ingredients except sour cream. Sprinkle top with parsley flakes.
Cover with lid and cook on low for 5-7 hours. Add sour cream
before serving, stirring well.

PARMESAN POTATOES

Prep. Time: about 15 minutes • Serves: 6 • Cost: about 42-cents per serving

8 large potatoes, peeled and sliced thin
¼ cup flour
¼ cup grated Parmesan cheese
1 teaspoon salt
¼ teaspoon black pepper
¼ cup butter
2 teaspoons dried parsley flakes
1 cup water

In small container, combine flour with Parmesan cheese, salt and pepper. Turn slow cooker on high and melt butter. Place a thin layer of sliced potatoes over bottom of slow cooker. Sprinkle with Parmesan cheese mixture. Add another layer of sliced potatoes and repeat sprinkling with Parmesan cheese. Continue until all potatoes and cheese has been used. Sprinkle parsley flakes over the top. Add cup of water. Cover with lid and cook on low for 5-7 hours.

SCALLOPED POTATOES

Prep. Time: about 15 minutes • Serves: 6 • Cost: about 47-cents per serving

8 medium potatoes, peeled and sliced
1 large onion, chopped
1½ teaspoons salt
¼ teaspoon black pepper
1 can cream of potato soup
1 cup milk

In slow cooker, combine sliced potatoes and chopped onion. Sprinkle the salt and pepper over the potatoes. Stir to blend well. In a separate container, mix together the condensed soup and the milk. Pour over the potatoes. Cover with lid and cook on high for a minimum of 5 hours.

'BAKED' POTATOES

Prep. Time: about 10 minutes • Serves: 6+ • Cost: about .15-cents per serving

6-8 medium white potatoes, scrubbed clean, left whole

Wrap each potato individually in aluminum foil. Stack wrapped potatoes in slow cooker. Cover with lid and cook on high for 6 hours or on low for 10 hours. Note: Do Not add any liquid to slow cooker with wrapped potatoes. As a result, the slow cooker will need little to no clean-up.

HARD-SHELLED SQUASH

Prep. Time: Less than 5 minutes • Serves: varies • Cost: about 10-15-cents per serving

Cook any hard-shelled squash (including small pumpkins) by placing squash in slow cooker. Cover with lid. Do not add any liquid. Cook on high setting for 5 hours or longer. Remove. Outer shell should peel right off, exposing the flesh. Cut in half to remove seeds. Season flesh and serve.

About The Author:

Penny E. Stone discovered the value of slow cooker cooking several years ago after experiencing severe back problems that left her almost bed-ridden. Over the coarse of three years and four back surgeries, Penny put a slow cooker manuscript together that featured all of the recipes you'll find in her Crazy About Slow Cookers *series. She shares her recipes and suggestions for using a slow cooker from the heart*

of experience. Penny resides in Indiana with her husband and three children. She is now active in her church, community, and as a professional author.

INDEX

Crazy About Crockery!

101 Soups & Stews for Less than .75¢ a serving

Penny E. Stone

Crazy About Crockery

101 Quick, Easy & Inexpensive Soup & Stew Recipes for Less than .75 Cents a Serving

Penny E. Stone

Also by Penny E. Stone

CRAZY ABOUT CROCKERY: 101 Soup & Stew Recipes for
Less than .75 cents a serving

CRAZY ABOUT CROCKERY: 101 Recipes for Entertaining at
 Less than .75 cents a serving

CRAZY ABOUT CROCKERY: 101 Easy & Inexpensive
 Recipes for Less than .75 cents a serving

365 Quick, Easy & Inexpensive Dinner Menus

CHAMPION PRESS, LTD.
FREDONIA, WISCONSIN

ISBN 1-891400-52-5 · LCCN 2002103113

Manufactured in Canada 10 9 8 7 6 5 4 3 2
Book Design by Kathy Campbell, Wildwood Studios

Introduction

Nothing warms the heart and soul like a good old-fashioned bowl of homemade soup. I consider soups, stews, and chowders to be "comfort food" because they're easy to make, nourishing to eat, and wonderful to share with family and friends. So put on a pot of soup and call in the family for a genuine time of togetherness.

For a complete recipe listing, please see page 102.

SECTION I

Soups

Cooking with a slow cooker can save you time and money all-year-long. In the summer I use mine to keep from heating up the kitchen and in the winter I set the steaming slow cooker on the table and we serve ourselves. When you prepare soups in the slow cooker, remember that a little seasoning will go along way. Because the flavors re-circulate within the slow cooker instead of evaporating during the cooking process, your food will taste richer and spicier than conventional cooking on the stove. There are some recipes that will actually taste better if you hold back adding the spices until the end of the cooking time. I've tried to make note of the recipes where I hold the spices until the end of cooking time—but you may find through your own experimentation what recipes work best for you by doing this.

Soups

HAM 'N' BEANS

Prep. Time: 15-20 minutes • Servings: 8+ • Cost: about 38-cents per serving

1 lb. dried soup beans
2 teaspoons baking soda
Water
2 tablespoons apple cider vinegar
1 tablespoon parsley flakes
1-2 smoked ham hocks or other ham seasoning
2 teaspoons salt

Wash one pound dried soup beans (navy, pinto, red, kidney, great northern, or a combination) and let soak in water overnight. The next morning, rinse beans again and put in large pan. Cover beans with water (end of finger to first knuckle) and bring to a fast boil. DO NOT ADD ANY SALT YET. When beans are boiling, transfer the pan to the sink and add two teaspoons of baking soda and stir. The water will turn green due to the baking soda. Drain the beans into a colander. Wash beans good in lukewarm water.

Put beans in fresh water in the slow cooker. Add water above beans, two tablespoons vinegar, one tablespoon parsley flakes, and either a smoked ham-hock or ham seasoning. Cook on high for six hours. Salt to taste when beans are cooked and ready to serve. (Salting beans before they are cooked makes them tough.)

For some variation, add chopped potatoes, carrots and onions and make this a stew. Or add a can of tomato soup to the slow cooker for a tomato-based ham 'n' beans. No soak method: wash one pound of beans and put in a large pan. Cover beans with water and bring to a boil on stove top. Follow the same procedure as above except turn slow cooker on low and cook for 12 to 14 hours.

BLACK BEAN SOUP

Prep. Time: 20 minutes • Servings: 8+ • Cost: about 41-cents per serving

1 lb. dried black beans
Water
2 teaspoons baking soda
1 smoked ham-hock
6 cups water
3 beef bouillon cubes
1 tablespoon olive oil
2 green bell peppers, finely chopped
2 large onions, finely chopped
1 clove garlic, finely minced
1 teaspoon ground cumin
1 can diced tomatoes with juice
¼ cup red wine vinegar
1 tablespoon fresh coriander, finely chopped

Wash dried beans and put them in a large soup pot. Cover with water and bring to a hard boil on stove top. Boil beans for about 5 minutes then transfer pan to sink. Drop in 2 teaspoons baking soda. This will make beans foam. Stir well and drain in colander. Rinse beans in cold water 2 times. Put rinsed beans in slow cooker. Add ham-hock, water, beef bouillon cubes, olive oil, and cumin. Cover with lid and cook on high for 6 hours. In a blender, combine chopped green pepper, chopped onion, minced garlic, diced tomatoes, red wine vinegar and fresh coriander. Puree contents. Pour pureed vegetables into slow cooker. Stir to blend well. Reduce heat to low, cover with lid and continue cooking for an additional 4 hours. Serve with a dollop of sour cream in the center of each bowl, if desired.

Chuck Wagon Beans

Prep. Time: about 15 minutes • Servings: 8+ • Cost: about 39-cents per serving

1-2 lbs. dry beans (use a variety of northern, red, pinto, etc.)
Water
2 teaspoons baking soda
1-2 smoked ham-hocks
1 lb. diced ham
1 large onion, chopped
6 cups water
5 white potatoes, peeled and cubed
2 carrots, sliced or diced
1 can (8 oz) tomato sauce

Wash beans thoroughly and drain in a colander. Put beans in a large soup pan and cover with water. Bring to a rapid boil on stove top and let boil for about 5 minutes. Transfer pan to sink and drop in 2 teaspoons of baking soda. This will cause beans to foam. Stir well and then rinse beans 2 -3 times, using a colander. Pour rinsed beans in slow cooker. Add 6 cups water, tomato sauce, diced ham, ham-hocks, and chopped onion. Cover with lid and cook on high for 5 hours. Add potatoes and carrots and continue cooking for an additional 4 hours on high.

Don't Treat Your Slow Cooker Like Corning®Ware!

A few years ago corning ware gained popularity for being very versatile. It could withstand extreme changes in temperatures and could go from the freezer, into the oven, and then onto the table. A slow cooker does not have this versatility. Extreme changes in temperatures will crack a slow cooker. Keep in mind slow cookers are clay based, so treat it with the same tenderness as your stoneware or pottery dishes.

SENATE BEAN SOUP

(this is a variation to what is served in the U.S. Senate dining room)

Prep. Time: 20 minutes • Servings: 8+ • Cost: about 42-cents per serving

1½ lbs. dried Navy beans
Water
2 teaspoons baking soda
8 - 10 cups water
1 smoked ham-bone or ham-hock
1 lb. smoked ham, cubed
2 large onions, finely chopped
3 stalks celery, finely chopped
2 cloves garlic, minced
4 medium potatoes, peeled and diced
2 teaspoons salt
½ teaspoon black pepper
4 sprigs fresh parsley, finely chopped

Put navy beans in large soup pan. Cover with water and bring to a fast boil on stove top. Let beans boil for about 5 minutes. Transfer pan to kitchen sink and add in 2 teaspoons baking soda. This will cause beans to foam. Stir to mix well. Rinse well in colander, at least twice. Place rinsed beans in slow cooker. Add 8 - 10 cups water and all remaining ingredients. Stir to blend well. Cover with lid and cook on high for 8 hours.

HOUSE OF REPRESENTATIVES BEAN SOUP

(this is a version of the bean soup served in the U.S. House of Representatives dining room)

Prep. Time: 15 minutes • Servings: 8 + • Cost: about 39-cents per serving

1½ lbs. dried Navy beans
Water
2 teaspoons baking soda
8 - 10 cups water
1 smoked ham-bone or ham-hock
1 lb. smoked ham, cubed
2 tablespoons cider vinegar
1 medium onion, finely chopped
2 teaspoons salt
½ teaspoon black pepper
4 sprigs fresh parsley, chopped fine

Put navy beans in large soup pan. Cover with water and bring to a fast boil on stove top. Let beans boil for about 5 minutes. Transfer pan to kitchen sink and add 2 teaspoons baking soda. This will cause beans to foam. Stir to mix well. Rinse well in colander, at least twice. Place rinsed beans in slow cooker. Add 8 - 10 cups water and all remaining ingredients. Stir to blend well. Cover with lid and cook on high for 8 hours.

ESAU'S SOUP

(This recipe is said to be the lineal descendant of the soup for which Esau sold his birthright. See Genesis 25 for the biblical story.)

Prep. Time: about 20 minutes • Servings: 6+ • Cost: about 65-cents per serving

1 lb. beef or venison stew meat, cut into small pieces
1 beef soup-bone
2 cups green split peas
1 cup red lentils
2 tablespoons pearl barley
½ to 1 cup white beans (navy, northern, etc.)
2 carrots, sliced
2 stalks celery, diced
1 onion, finely chopped
1-2 cloves garlic
2 bay leaves
Water
Salt and pepper to taste

Soak peas, lentils, barley and beans overnight in cold water. Rinse and drain, then add to the slow cooker. Add all remaining ingredients, except for the salt and pepper. Fill slow cooker with water. Cover and cook on high for 6-8 hours. Remove beef bone, garlic and bay leaves before serving. Season to taste.

BEEF CHUCK SOUP

Prep. Time: 15-20 minutes • Servings: 8+ • Cost: about 44-cents per serving

1 lb. or more beef chuck roast
5 cups water
3 beef bouillon cubes
1 teaspoon Worcestershire sauce™
½ teaspoon sweet basil
1 teaspoon chopped chives
2 bay leaves
2 teaspoons salt
½ teaspoon pepper
4 fresh meaty tomatoes, skins removed OR
2 cups canned stewed tomatoes, cut up
¼ cup barley
3 large carrots, sliced
2 stalks celery, sliced
1 onion, chopped
1 teaspoon minced garlic

Combine all ingredients in slow cooker. Cover with lid and cook on high for 6 hours. Remove meat and cut into pieces. Add back to slow cooker. Add tomato juice or water if soup does not have enough liquid to suit your tastes. Adjust seasonings according to your taste. Check vegetables for tenderness. May need to cook 1 to 2 hours longer, depending upon how soft you like your vegetables.

STONE SOUP

Author's Note: After reading the children's story by this title, I decided it was an appropriate title for my homemade vegetable and beef soup.

Prep. Time: about 15 minutes • Servings: 8+ • Cost: about 69-cents per serving

1 quart water
2 teaspoons salt, more to taste if desired
1 teaspoon dried basil
1 teaspoon dried parsley
½ teaspoon coarse black pepper
1 smooth stone, scrubbed clean, optional—(large enough not to be
    accidentally eaten!)
1 medium onion, chopped
6-8 medium potatoes, peeled and cubed
4 medium carrots, chopped
1 stalk celery, chopped
1 lb. beef stew meat, cut in cubes
2 cups green beans
1 cup sweet corn
For variation add 1 or more of the following:
1 cup sweet peas
1 cup beans, any variety
1 cup lentils
1 cup dried split peas
2 cups chopped ripe tomatoes
1 med. zucchini, chopped
1 large summer squash, chopped

Combine all ingredients in slow cooker. Stir to blend well. Cover with lid and cook on high for 5-6 hours or reduce heat to low and let cook for 7-8 hours. When dipping up the soup, drop the stone in someone's bowl and add soup over it. Serve. Whoever finds a stone in his bowl will have good luck. DO NOT EAT THE STONE!

Oxtail Soup

Prep. Time: 15-20 minutes • Servings: 8+ • Cost: about 65-cents per serving

1 lb. oxtail joints with meat
1 cup flour
2 teaspoons salt
½ teaspoon black pepper
Hot oil
4 cups water
1 teaspoon salt
½ teaspoon pepper
3 allspice berries (whole)
2 stalks celery, sliced
4 carrots, sliced
1 onion, chopped
2 tablespoons chopped parsley
1 tablespoon Worcestershire sauce™
1 cup shredded aged cheese
2 cups dried seasoned croutons

Combine flour with 2 teaspoons salt and ½ teaspoon pepper. Roll oxtail joints in flour. Heat oil in a large, deep kettle and deep fry the oxtail joints until lightly browned. Remove from oil and drain. In slow cooker, combine water with 1 teaspoon salt, ½ teaspoon pepper, allspice berries, sliced celery, carrots, chopped onion, and Worcestershire sauce™. Add oxtail joints. Cover with lid and cook on high for 6 hours. Remove oxtail joints and set aside to slightly cool. Skim top of soup with cheesecloth and discard. Pick meat from bones and return meat to slow cooker. Discard bones. Stir to blend well. Serve with shredded cheese and seasoned croutons over top of each serving.

PENNY'S CHILI

Author's Note: This chili won the award for being the mildest chili in the Red Gold Chili Cook-off of 2001. It is a full-flavored yet mild chili for those of us who prefer not to experience heartburn with our chili.

Prep. Time: 15-20 minutes • Servings: 8+ • Cost: about 45-cents per serving

1 lb. lean ground beef or turkey

1 medium onion, finely chopped

2 cups cooked elbow macaroni

1 quart tomato juice

1 pint stewed tomatoes

2 cans (15.5 oz) red beans

3 tablespoons chili powder, add more or less to taste

½ to 1 teaspoon cumin (start with the ½ teaspoon)

1 tablespoon salt, add more or less to taste

1 teaspoon garlic powder

2 teaspoons dried basil

2 teaspoons dried oregano

3-6 cups water, depending upon how "soupy" you want it

In skillet, brown ground meat with chopped onion. When meat is cooked, drain off all grease. Crumble meat and onion into slow cooker. Combine all ingredients except for macaroni in slow cooker and stir to blend well. When adding the stewed tomatoes, slice the tomatoes with a knife into bite-sized chunks. Cover with lid and cook on low for 6 - 8 hours. Prepare macaroni according to package directions. Rinse in cold water to stop cooking action. Add drained pasta to chili and stir well to blend; then serve.

CUBAN CHILI CON CARNE

Prep. Time: 15-2...........0 minutes • Servings: 8+ • Cost: about 57-cents per serving

1 lb. lean ground beef or turkey
2 large onions, chopped
1 stalk celery, diced
1 green pepper, diced
2 large cans stewed tomatoes
2 cans red kidney beans with liquid
1 clove garlic
2 tablespoons chili powder, add more to taste
2 teaspoons salt, add more to taste
½ teaspoon cumin, add more to taste
½ teaspoon pepper, add more to taste

Brown meat and onions in large skillet. Drain off all grease. Crumble meat and onions into slow cooker. Add all remaining ingredients. Cover with lid and cook on low for 5-7 hours.

Don't Re-Warm Soup in the Slow Cooker

It's okay to serve soups or stews directly from the slow cooker when dinner is ready, and it's even okay to put the lid on the slow cooker and set it in the refrigerator. But it's not okay to take the slow cooker out of the fridge and return it to the heating unit to re-warm the contents. There's two reasons why this is not a good idea. First, the drastic change in temperature between the refrigerator and heating unit is enough to crack the slow cooker. And second, by cooking, storing, and reheating within the same container, you're inviting bacteria to grow which can cause food poisoning. So always reheat your soups or stews in a pan on the stove or use a microwave safe container and zap it in the microwave.

TRADITIONAL GROCERY-STORE CHILI

Prep. Time: about 15 minutes • Servings: 6+ • Cost: about 68-cents per serving

1 lb. lean ground beef or turkey
1 onion, chopped
2 large cans (Brooks™ or American™ chili beans with seasoning
1 cup water

In skillet, brown meat with chopped onions. When meat is cooked, drain off all grease. Crumble meat into slow cooker. Add remaining ingredients and stir to blend well. Cover with lid and cook on low for 4 hours or longer.

Spicy Chili Lentil Soup

Prep. Time: about 15 minutes • Servings: 6+ • Cost: about 69-cents per serving

2 lbs. washed lentils
Water
2 teaspoons baking soda
8 cups water
2 beef bouillon cubes or 2 teaspoons beef seasoning mix
2 stalks celery, diced
1 large onion, finely chopped
4 carrots, diced
1 clove garlic, minced
1 quart stewed tomatoes with juice
½ teaspoon cayenne pepper
1 teaspoon ground cumin
1 tablespoon chili powder
2 teaspoons salt
1 cup barley

Wash and rinse lentils thoroughly. Put lentils in a large soup pan and cover with water. Bring lentils to a fast boil on stove top and boil for about 5 minutes. Transfer pot from stove to sink. Add 2 teaspoons baking soda in pot. This will cause lentils to foam. Stir to mix well and then rinse lentils in colander at least twice. Transfer rinsed lentils to slow cooker. Add 8 cups water and beef bouillon. Stir until bouillon is dissolved. Add diced celery, chopped onion, diced carrots, garlic, stewed tomatoes, barley and seasonings. Stir to blend well. Cover with lid and cook on high for 8 hours.

CHILI CHOCOLATE SURPRISE

Prep. Time: about 20 minutes • Servings: 8+ • Cost: about 74-cents per serving

2 lbs. lean ground beef or turkey, browned and drained
1 large onion, chopped
1 medium green pepper, chopped
2 teaspoons salt
2 tablespoons chili powder
1 teaspoon black pepper
2 teaspoons cumin
½ teaspoon allspice
1 quart stewed tomatoes with juice
2 cans red kidney beans
2 tablespoons sugar
2 oz semisweet chocolate
1 bay leaf
1 can (4 oz.) tomato paste
1 large can beef broth

Brown meat in skillet with chopped onions and green pepper. Drain off all grease and crumble meat in slow cooker. Add all remaining ingredients to slow cooker. Stir to blend well. Cover with lid and cook on low for 8 hours. Remove bay leaf before serving.

CREAM OF CARROT SOUP

Prep. Time: about 20 minutes • Servings: 6+ • Cost: about 48-cents per serving

8-10 med. to large carrots, sliced
1-2 cups diced celery
3 med. to large white potatoes, peeled and diced
6 cups canned chicken broth
1 pint heavy cream
Dash nutmeg
Salt and pepper according to taste

Finely grate all the carrots. Reserve 1 cup grated carrot, but put the remaining in slow cooker. Combine diced celery, diced potatoes, chicken broth and 1 teaspoon salt in slow cooker. Cover with lid and cook on high for 4-6 hours. Turn heat off and let contents cool. Transfer 2 cups vegetables with broth to blender and puree, return mixture toslow cooker. Continue until all vegetables have been pureed. Add heavy cream and adjust seasonings according to taste. Add reserved grated carrot. Cover with lid, reduce heat to low, and continue cooking for 2-3 hours. Sprinkle a dash of nutmeg over each serving.

CREAM OF CELERY SOUP

Prep. Time: about 20 minutes • Servings: 6+ • Cost: about 49-cents per serving

4 cups chopped celery (use inner stalks of the lighter colored celery
  for best results)
1 large onion, chopped
6 cups chicken broth
2 cups half and half or heavy cream
3 tablespoons butter or margarine
2 tablespoons cornstarch dissolved in½ cup cool water
½ teaspoon salt, add more according to taste
¼ teaspoon pepper, add more according to taste

In slow cooker combine 3 cups chopped celery with half of the chopped onion and all of the chicken broth. Cover with lid and cook on high for 6-7 hours. After cooking 6-7 hours, in skillet melt butter or margarine and saute remaining chopped onion and 1 cup chopped celery until vegetables become tender. Add cornstarch water and 2 cups half and half or heavy cream. Continue stirring over medium heat until mixture begins to thicken and boil. Remove contents from slow cooker and combine vegetables and broth in blender to puree. Combine pureed vegetables/broth with hot gravy mixture in slow cooker. Add salt and pepper and adjust seasonings according to taste. Cover with lid, reduce heat to low, and continue cooking 2-3 hours to allow flavors to blend.

CREAM OF MUSHROOM SOUP

Prep. Time: about 20 minutes • Servings: 6+ • Cost: about 72-cents per serving

1 lb. fresh mushrooms, chopped fine
1 med. onion, chopped fine
3 tablespoons butter or margarine
2 cans evaporated milk
2 tablespoons cornstarch dissolved in½ cup cool water
2 small cans chicken broth
1 pint heavy cream
½ teaspoon salt, add more according to taste
¼ teaspoon black pepper, add more according to taste

In skillet over medium heat melt butter or margarine and saute chopped onion and ¾ cup chopped mushrooms until vegetables are tender. Add evaporated milk and cornstarch water. Continue cooking and stirring over medium heat until mixture begins to boil and thicken. Pour gravy mixture into slow cooker. Add chicken broth and half of the remaining chopped mushrooms, salt and pepper. Adjust seasonings according to taste. Cover with lid and cook on low for 4-6 hours. After cooking, add heavy cream and remaining chopped mushrooms. Stir to blend well. Cover and continue cooking for 1 hour then serve hot from the slow cooker.

VERA'S TUNA CHEESE SOUP

Author's Note: If you pass on preparing this soup based on its name, then you're missing a real treat! A dear friend of mine invited me to join her for lunch at her house one winter afternoon. We walked the four blocks from work and when we arrived, the soup was ready in her slow cooker. She served it with some fresh French bread and it was so good! I encourage you to try this recipe before you pass judgement. I'm positive you'll be pleasantly surprised, as I was!

Prep. Time: about 15 minutes • Servings: 6+ • Cost: about 57-cents per serving

1 large onion, finely chopped
1 green pepper, finely chopped
2 stalks celery, finely diced
¼ cup butter
2 cans cheddar cheese soup
2 soup cans milk
1 small can stewed tomatoes, cut in small pieces
2 small cans tuna, drained
2½ cups uncooked instant rice

In large pan saute onion and green pepper and celery in butter or margarine until tender. Add two cans of cheddar cheese soup plus two cans of milk and stir until heated. Transfer vegetables and soup to slow cooker. Add one small can of stewed tomatoes cut into small pieces and two cans of tuna, drained and flaked. Cook on low for at least two hours. When ready to serve, add two and a half cups of instant rice. Cover until rice is cooked and then serve hot. This is especially good when served with warm French break, hot garlic bread, or rolls.

◉ HAM SEASONED PEA SOUP

Prep. Time: about 20 minutes • Servings: 6+ • Cost: about 48-cents per serving

1 lb. dry green split peas, rinsed well
2 quarts water
½ to 1-lb. ham, cubed or diced
1 smoked ham-hock
6 to 8 medium potatoes, peeled and cubed
1 large onion, chopped
½ teaspoon garlic powder
2 teaspoons salt
½ teaspoon dried marjoram, crushed
½ teaspoon black pepper
1 cup chopped celery
1 cup chopped carrot

Pour water into slow cooker. Add split peas, smoked ham hock, chopped onion, celery and carrot. Cover with lid and cook on high for 5 hours. Add all remaining ingredients and stir to blend well. Cover with lid and continue cooking on high for 3 to 4 additional hours. Remove smoked ham-hock before serving.

CHEESE SOUP WITH ITSY-BITSY POTATOES

Prep. Time: about 20 minutes • Servings: 8+ • Cost: about 48-cents per serving

4 beef bouillon cubes of 2 tablespoons beef seasoning mix
6 cups water
1 onion, finely chopped
2 stalks celery, finely chopped
1 teaspoon salt
¼ teaspoon black pepper
2 cans evaporated milk
2 teaspoons cornstarch dissolved in 1/3 cup water
2 cans cheddar cheese soup
1 lb. American cheese, cubed
Do last:
10 medium potatoes, peeled and quartered. Cut each quarter into a
    quarter and dice potatoes.

Heat water until hot then add bouillon; stir until dissolved. Pour beef-water into slow cooker. Add celery, onion, salt and pepper. Stir in evaporated milk, cornstarch water, and cheddar cheese soups. Add diced potatoes. Cover with lid and cook on low for 6-8 hours. Add cheese cubes during last hour of cooking time. Stir before serving.

VEGGIE POTATO SOUP

Prep. Time: about 15 minutes • Servings: 6+ • Cost: about 49-cents per serving

6-8 potatoes, peeled and cubed
2 small to medium yellow onions, peeled and left whole
2 stalks celery, cut in thirds
2 carrots, sliced
1 tablespoon dried parsley flakes
2 teaspoons salt
½ teaspoon pepper
5 cups water
4 chicken bouillon cubes or 2 tablespoons chicken seasoning mix
2 cups milk
2 teaspoons cornstarch dissolved in ½ cup cool water

In slow cooker, combine cubed potatoes with onions, celery chunks, carrots, parsley flakes, salt, pepper, water and chicken bouillon. Stir to blend well. Cover with lid and cook on high for 6 hours. Scoop out cooked celery and onion with about a cup of soup broth and place in blender. Add cold milk and cornstarch water. Whiz on high until vegetables are pureed. Pour contents back into slow cooker. Stir to blend well. Reduce heat to low and let simmer to thicken until ready to serve.

No Need for Reconstituting Dehydrated Foods

Normally when you cook with dehydrated onions or raisins, you know to soak them in warm water and re-hydrate them before adding them to your recipe. But when cooking in a slow cooker, you can skip this step and add the dried ingredients directly to the slow cooker with your recipe's other ingredients. Since the slow cooker generates moisture as it cooks, and that moisture gets re-circulated continuously within the slow cooker—those dried foods will automatically re-hydrate on their own.

PENNY'S CHEESY POTATO SOUP WITH DUMPLINGS

Prep. Time: about 15 minutes • Servings: 8+ • Cost: about 53-cents per serving

10 potatoes, peeled and cut in large cubes
2 stalks celery, cut in thirds
2 small to medium yellow onions, left whole
2 teaspoons salt
½ teaspoon pepper
4 cups water
2 cups milk
1 tablespoon cornstarch
1 lb. American cheese, cubed
1 cup cheddar cheese cubes
  Egg Dumplings:
1 cup flour
2 eggs
½ teaspoon salt

Combine potatoes, celery, onions, 2 teaspoons salt, ½ teaspoon pepper, and 4 cups water in slow cooker. Cover with lid and cook on high for 6 hours. Remove from slow cooker 1 onion and half of the celery with about ½ cup broth and put in blender. Add 1 cup cold milk and 1 tablespoon cornstarch. Whiz on high to puree vegetables. Pour broth back into slow cooker. Remove from slow cooker the remaining onion and celery and add the second cup of milk. Whiz on high to puree and pour broth back into slow cooker. Add both cheeses. Reduce heat to low and cover with lid. Continue cooking for another 2 hours. In a separate container, combine flour, ½ teaspoon salt and eggs. Mix with a fork until mixture forms a wet dough. With a teaspoon, drop dough into the boiling broth of soup. These make the dumplings and they will float on top when cooked. Be careful not to make dumplings too large as they will not cook all the way through when dropped in the soup. Do not cover with a lid after adding dumplings. Let dumplings cook in hot soup for about 30 minutes before serving.

Mama's Old Fashioned Potato Soup with Dumplings

Prep. Time: about 15 minutes • Servings: 8+ • Cost: about 51-cents per serving

10 - 12 potatoes, peeled and cubed
2 - 3 stalks of celery, diced
1 medium onion, finely chopped
Water
1- 2 quarts milk
3 tablespoons butter or margarine
¾ cup flour
2 teaspoons salt
½ teaspoon pepper
  Egg Dumplings
2 eggs, lightly beaten
1 cup flour
½ teaspoon salt
¼ teaspoon pepper

Peel potatoes and cube them. Dice celery and onion and add to potatoes in slow cooker. Sprinkle 2 teaspoons salt and½ teaspoon pepper over vegetables. Add 2 - 3 cups water. Cover with lid and cook on high for 5 hours. On stove top in skillet, melt butter and stir in ¾ cup flour to make a paste. Add cold milk and continue stirring over medium heat until mixture thickens. Pour skillet mixture into slow cooker and stir. In separate container, combine beaten eggs salt and pepper, then add enough flour to make a stiff dough. Spoon drops of egg-dough into boiling hot soup. Do not cover with a lid after adding dumplings. Let dumplings cook in hot soup for about 30 minutes before serving.

AMISH CHICKEN NOODLE SOUP

Prep. Time: about 20-30 minutes • Servings: 8+ • Cost: about 61-cents per serving

1 chicken, cut up
Water
1 teaspoon salt
½ teaspoon pepper
1 teaspoon poultry seasoning
½ teaspoon sweet basil
1 teaspoon parsley flakes
1 bay leaf
3 cups diced celery
5 cups diced potatoes
3 cups diced carrots
1 teaspoon salt
½ teaspoon pepper
4 cups cooked noodles

Wash chicken. Place chicken in slow cooker and cover with water. Add 1 teaspoon salt, ½ teaspoon pepper, poultry seasoning, basil, parsley flakes and bay leaf. Cover with lid and cook on high for 4 hours. Remove meat from slow cooker and set aside. Pour chicken broth through sieve (or a clean coffee filter). Return pure broth back to slow cooker. Add vegetables with 1 teaspoon salt and ½ teaspoon pepper. Cover with lid and let cook on high while picking chicken off the bone. Add chicken pieces to slow cooker and stir. Cover with lid, reduce heat to low, and cook for 4 more hours or longer, depending upon how tender you want the vegetables. When vegetables are cooked to the desired doneness, add noodles and stir to blend well. Ladle out soup into bowls.

TURKEY AND WILD RICE SOUP

Prep. Time: about 15-20 minutes • Servings: 8+ • Cost: about 57-cents per serving

2 quarts clear chicken broth
1 cup uncooked white rice
½ cup uncooked wild rice
1 bunch green onions, chopped fine, green tops included
3 tablespoons butter
½ cup flour
1 teaspoon salt
½ teaspoon black pepper
1 pint half and half or heavy cream
3 cups cooked turkey pieces, dark and white meat
½ teaspoon sweet basil
½ teaspoon thyme

In skillet, melt butter and saute green onions for about 5 minutes. Add flour and stir to make a paste. Pour in one quart of chicken broth and stir constantly until sauce thickens. Pour thickened sauce into slow cooker. Add remaining quart of chicken broth, turkey meat, white and wild rice, salt, pepper, basil and thyme. Stir to blend well. Cover with lid and cook on high for 6 hours or on low for 9 hours. Add heavy cream just prior to serving; stir to blend well.

HEARTY TOMATO SOUP

Prep. Time: about 20 minutes • Servings: 8+ • Cost: about 54-cents per serving

3-4 meaty tomatoes, skins removed, chopped
2 quarts stewed tomatoes with juice
1 onion, quartered
1 small green pepper, quartered
1 teaspoon parsley flakes
1 bay leaf
3 whole cloves
1 tablespoon salt
½ cup brown sugar
2 tablespoons cornstarch dissolved in ½ cup water
½ teaspoon ground sage
2 tablespoons butter
3 cups water

Pour 3 cups water in slow cooker. Add onion, green pepper, bay leaf, and whole cloves. Cover with lid and cook on high for 3 hours. OR bring this combination to a boil on stove top and continue cooking until vegetables are tender. Strain broth and pour clear juices into slow cooker. The cooked onion and green pepper may be pureed and added back to the slow cooker or discarded, depending upon taste preferences. Discard cloves after cooking. In a separate pan, combine stewed tomatoes and juice with brown sugar, salt, and sage and bring mixture to a slow boil over medium heat. When mixture begins bubbling around outer sides, add cornstarch water. Continue stirring and cooking over medium heat until mixture thickens. Pour thickened tomato mixture into slow cooker. Add the fresh diced tomatoes and stir. Cover with lid and cook on low for 4 hours or longer. This soup goes great with toasted cheese sandwiches!

HARVEST SOUP

Prep. Time: about 20 minutes • Servings: 8+ • Cost: about 60-cents per serving, less if you grow your own vegetables!

4 carrots, sliced
6-8 small to med. potatoes, peeled and cubed
2 stalks celery, diced
1 large or 2 small to med. onions, chopped
½ cup chopped green pepper, optional
2 cans or 1 pint green beans, drained
1 can whole kernel corn, drained
1 can baby peas, drained
¼ cup brown sugar
1 quart V-8 juice™
1 lb. diced ham OR beef stew meat
2 teaspoons salt
½ teaspoon pepper

Combine all ingredients in slow cooker. Cover with lid and cook on high for 6-7 hours.

ONION SOUP

Prep. Time: about 15 minutes • Servings: 6+ • Cost: about 29-cents per serving

5 small yellow onions, peeled and thinly sliced
2 teaspoons sugar
2 tablespoons cornstarch
2-3 pints clear beef stock
1½ tablespoons butter or margarine

Turn slow cooker on high. Melt butter and add onions. Let onions cook, uncovered, for up to 1 hour, stirring occasionally. Stir in sugar. Dissolve cornstarch in beef stock and slowly add to slow cooker. Stir to mix well. Cover with lid and reduce heat to low. Cook for 6-7 hours. Serve with toasted croutons or bread rolls.

FRENCH ONION SOUP

Prep. Time: about 20 minutes • Servings: 6+ • Cost: about 43-cents per serving

2 large onions
2 tablespoons cornstarch
½ cup cold water
3 cans (10.5 oz) beef broth
1 teaspoon salt
½ cup half and half
1 egg yolk, beaten
2 teaspoons Worcestershire sauce™
Swiss Cheese slices
French Bread, toasted

Peel and slice onions into rings. Put onions in slow cooker. Add beef broth and salt. Cover with lid and cook on high for about 4 hours. Next, beat egg yolk and stir in half and half. Add Worcestershire sauce TM and stir well. Pour this egg and cream mixture into slow cooker. Cover with lid and let cook for another 2 hours. In a separate container, dissolve cornstarch in ½ cup water. Pour this into the slow cooker. Stir to blend well. Cover with lid and reduce heat to low until ready to serve. Serve by placing a slice of Swiss cheese in the bottom of each bowl. Ladle hot soup into bowl. Add another slice of cheese on top. Serve with toasted French Bread.

AMERICAN MINESTRONE

Prep. Time: about 20 minutes • Servings: 8+ • Cost: about 58-cents per serving

1 - 2 lbs. beef stew meat, cut into small pieces
2 medium onions, finely chopped
1 teaspoon minced garlic
1 medium zucchini, diced in cubes
2 stalks celery, sliced or diced
1 can (28 oz) tomatoes, cut, undrained
1 can (15 oz) kidney beans, undrained
1 can sweet kernel corn, undrained
2 cups water, boiling
2 teaspoons salt
2 teaspoons Italian seasoning
3 beef bouillon cubes
1 cup uncooked small elbow macaroni pasta
Parmesan cheese

Dissolve bouillon cubes in boiling water. Combine all ingredients in slow cooker except the elbow macaroni and Parmesan cheese. Stir to blend well. Cover with lid and cook on high for 5 hours. Remove lid and add uncooked pasta. Stir to blend well. Let soup cook about 30-45 minutes longer, uncovered, to cook pasta. Serve with Parmesan cheese.

SECTION II

Stews

Coming home to a homemade pot of stew is as enticing as it is nourishing. At my house, if we have leftover stew after a meal, we prepare individual servings in freezer containers and have ready-made "lunches to go" that can be zapped in the microwave and eaten on the job. This helps to stretch our food budget considerably. I hope you enjoy these stew recipes.

LUCK OF THE IRISH STEW

Prep. Time: about 15 minutes • Serves: 6+   Cost: about 68-cents per serving

2-3 lbs. beef stew meat, cut in small pieces
3 tablespoons oil
½ to 1 cup flour
2½ cups water
1 quart beef broth
6-8 carrots
About 15 new red potatoes, scrubbed clean and cut in quarters
2 large sweet onions, chopped
1 cup dry red wine
1 clove garlic, minced
1 teaspoon salt
½ teaspoon pepper
¼ teaspoon dried thyme
2 bay leaves

In bowl combine red wine, minced garlic, salt, pepper, and dried thyme. Add meat and make sure all meat gets coated with wine mixture. Set bowl in refrigerator to marinade for at least 3 hours, preferably overnight. Drain beef, reserving marinade. Put flour in baggie and drop meat into bag, shake to cover each piece of meat. Heat oil in skillet and brown floured meat until browned on all sides. Drain meat and place in slow cooker. Add all remaining ingredients including reserved marinade to slow cooker. Cover with lid and cook on low for 7-9 hours. Remove bay leaves before serving.

RISING HEAT COWBOY STEW

Prep. Time: about 10 minutes • Serves: 6+ • Cost:
about 65-cents per serving

1-2 lbs. beef stew meat, cut into small pieces
1 small can (10.5 oz.) beef broth
1 can stewed tomatoes with liquid
1 jar (8 oz.) picante sauce, your choice as to mild, medium, hot or
   extra hot
1 pkg. (10-oz.) frozen whole-kernel corn, thawed
4 carrots, sliced
1 large onion, chopped
2 cloves garlic, minced
2 jalapeno peppers, seeds removed, chopped—optional
1 teaspoon ground cumin
1 teaspoon salt
2 tablespoons cornstarch dissolved in½ cup cool water

Combine all ingredients in slow cooker except cornstarch water.
Cover with lid and cook on high for 5 hours or on low for 8-10 hours.
An hour before serving, add cornstarch water and stir to blend well.
Return lid to slow cooker and continue cooking for that last hour.

CHILI CON CARNE STEW

Prep. Time: about 20 minutes • Serves: 6 • Cost: about 57-cents per serving

1-2 lbs. lean ground beef
2 med. onions, chopped
½ teaspoon salt
1 small to med. green bell pepper, chopped
1 clove garlic, minced
1 can (16 oz.) stewed tomatoes with juice
2 cans (16 oz.) red kidney beans, undrained
1 qt. tomato juice
2 teaspoons chili powder
1 teaspoon ground cumin
½ teaspoon dried basil
½ teaspoon dried oregano
2 small cans (4 oz.) red or green chilies, chopped
2 teaspoons salt
½ teaspoon pepper

In skillet, cook meat with onion, garlic, and ½ teaspoon salt sprinkled over all. Drain meat and discard grease. Transfer meat and vegetables to slow cooker. Add all remaining ingredients and stir to blend well. Cover with lid and cook on low for 7-9 hours.

BUTCHER STEW

Prep. Time: about 15 minutes • Serves: 6 • Cost: about 48-cents per serving

1 lb. beef liver
2 tablespoons shortening
¼ cup flour
5-8 potatoes, peeled and cubed
3-4 carrots, peeled and sliced
1 large onion, finely chopped
1 teaspoon salt
¼ teaspoon pepper
Water
Ketchup
Oil or shortening

Flour and brown liver in oil or shortening. Remove from pan and place in slow cooker. Add vegetables, salt, and pepper. Add enough water to almost cover the meat. Cover contents with ketchup. Cover with lid and cook on high for 6 hours. Meat should fall apart when you're ready to serve. If it doesn't, gently cut meat in slow cooker before serving.

APPLE STEW

Prep. Time: about 15 minutes • Serves: 8+ • Cost: about 63-cents per serving

2 lbs. beef stew meat, cut into pieces
¼ to ½ cup flour
1 teaspoon salt
½ teaspoon pepper
¼ teaspoon dried thyme
3 tablespoons oil
3 cups unsweetened apple juice
2 cups water
2 tablespoons apple cider vinegar
6-8 new red potatoes, scrubbed clean and cubed
4 carrots, sliced
1 onion, chopped
1 stalk celery, chopped

Heat oil in skillet. In plastic bag, combine flour, 1 teaspoon salt, ½ teaspoon pepper, and thyme. Add meat a few pieces at a time and shake to evenly coat. Transfer meat to hot oil and lightly brown meat on all sides. Remove meat and put in slow cooker. Add onion and celery and cook until onion turns transparent. Add to slow cooker. Combine all remaining ingredients in slow cooker. Cover with lid and cook on low for 7 hours. Adjust seasonings according to taste and serve.

HOMEMADE BEEF STEW

Prep. Time: about 15 minutes • Serves: 8+ • Cost: about 53-cents per serving

2 lbs. stewing beef or leftover roast, torn in pieces
1 can (8 oz.) tomato sauce
4 beef bouillon cubes
1 quart water
1 onion, halved
2 stalks celery, cut in thirds
8-10 potatoes, peeled and cubed
4-5 carrots, sliced
1 teaspoon salt
½ teaspoon pepper
2 teaspoons cornstarch dissolved in½ cup cool water

Combine all ingredients in slow cooker and cover with lid. Cook on high for 6 hours. Remove onion halves and celery pieces with about a cup of broth and put in blender. Whiz on high to puree vegetables. Dissolve cornstarch in half cup cool water and pour into blender. Whiz again to mix well. Pour pureed vegetables back in slow cooker. Stir to blend well. Cover and let cook for another 2 hours then serve.

EASY BEEF STEW

Prep. Time: about 10 minutes • Serves: 6 • Cost: about 49-cents per serving

2 lbs. stew beef, cubed
2 teaspoons salt
2 bay leaves
¼ teaspoon pepper
2 stalks celery, diced
2 onions, diced
4 carrots, sliced
6 potatoes, peeled and cubed
2 cans tomato soup
2 soup cans water

Combine all ingredients in slow cooker; stir to blend well. Cover with lid and cook on low for 7-9 hours. Remove bay leaves before serving.

CREAMY ONION BEEF STEW

Prep. Time: about 10 minutes • Serves: 6+ • Cost: about 69-cents per serving

2 lbs. stewing beef or leftover roast, torn in pieces
1 pkg. dried onion soup mix
2 large onions, chopped
2 cups water with 3 beef bouillon cubes dissolved
1 can cream of mushroom soup
1 can cream of onion soup
6-8 potatoes, peeled and cubed
4-6 carrots, sliced or chunked
2-3 stalks of celery, sliced or diced

Combine all ingredients and stir to blend well. Cover with lid and cook on high for 6 hours or on low for 9 hours. Stir before serving.

"Clean Out the Freezer" Stew

Prep. Time: about 15 minutes • Serves: 6+ • Cost: about 58-cents per serving

2 lbs. stewing beef or leftover roast, torn in pieces

1 (10 oz.) bag of sliced frozen carrots or the equivalent leftover
    carrots

1 (10 oz.) bag of frozen peas and onions or the equivalent leftover
    peas with onions added

1 (10 oz.) bag of frozen corn or the equivalent leftover corn

1 (8 oz.) can tomato sauce

1 can cream of mushroom soup

1 can cream of celery soup

2 soup cans water

1 tablespoon Worcestershire sauce™

½ cup ketchup

2 teaspoons salt

½ teaspoon pepper

1 teaspoon dried parsley flakes

1 teaspoon dried chives

1 teaspoon garlic powder

½ teaspoon dried sweet basil

½ teaspoon dried oregano

Set aside bags of frozen vegetables. Combine all remaining ingredients and stir to blend well. Then add bags of semi-frozen vegetables, stirring to blend after each addition. Cover with lid and cook on high for 6 hours or on low for 9 hours.

FRENCH OVEN STEW

Prep. Time: about 15 minutes • Serves: 8+ • Cost: about 62-cents per serving

2 lbs. beef stew meat, in cubes or small chunks
2 medium onions, cut in quarters
3 stalks celery, cut in pieces
4 medium carrots, cut in half
1 quart stewed tomatoes with juice
½ cup quick cooking tapioca
1 tablespoon sugar
2 teaspoons salt
½ teaspoon coarse black pepper
1 teaspoon basil
1 teaspoon parsley
10-14 red potatoes, scrubbed clean

Combine all ingredients in slow cooker. Cover with lid and cook on low for 7-9 hours. Remove onion quarters and celery pieces with a little liquid and puree in blender, then return to slow cooker. Stir to blend well before serving.

BEEF BURGUNDY STEW

Prep. Time: about 20 minutes • Serves: 6 • Cost: about 65-cents per serving

2 lbs. round steak or stew meat, cubed
2 medium onions, chopped
1½ cups water
1 small can mushrooms, drained
2 tablespoons butter
2 tablespoons cooking sherry
¼ cup tomato paste
3 tablespoons flour
1 cup onion juice—see directions below
½ cup red wine
1 teaspoon salt
¼ teaspoon pepper

In small saucepan, add 1½ cups water to chopped onions and bring to a boil. Let boil for about 5 minutes and then remove from heat. In skillet, melt butter and brown meat lightly. Add flour and stir to form a paste, then add onion juice and tomato paste to make a gravy. Stir to blend well. Pour gravy and meat into slow cooker. Add all remaining ingredients and stir to blend well. Cover with lid and cook on low for 7-9 hours. Serve meat and sauce over cooked rice, noodles or baked potatoes.

HAMBURGER STEW

1 lb. lean ground beef or ground round
1 large can tomato juice
1 onion, chopped
8-12 potatoes, peeled and diced
1 pkg. (10 oz.) frozen corn, thawed
1 pkg. (10 oz.) frozen green beans, thawed
1 pkg. (10 oz.) frozen carrots, thawed
1 pkg. (10 oz.) frozen peas, thawed
1 teaspoon salt, add more to taste
½ teaspoon pepper, add more to taste
Water, as needed

In skillet over medium heat, cook hamburger with chopped onion until done. Drain and crumble meat into slow cooker. Add all remaining ingredients. Add water to desired Asoupiness@. Cover with lid and cook on low for 6-9 hours. Stir well before serving.

Maximizing Freezer Space

If you have leftover soup after making up a slow cooker full, here's how you can freeze it and still maximize your freezer space. This suggestion comes originally from Debi Taylor-Hough, the author of Frozen Assets. Take an empty cereal box or large coffee can and line it with a gallon sized freezer bag. Pour your leftover soup into the bag. Seal, then lay flat on a cookie sheet in your freezer until the contents are frozen. This will cause the soup to freeze in the shape of a flat book. Once it's frozen, you can stack the bags either vertically or horizontally, one next to the other. I'd like to add one modification to Debi's suggestion though. Don't pour boiling hot soup directly from the slow cooker into the freezer bag. It might melt a hole in the bag! Instead, let the hot soup cool until that danger is passed and then pour it into the freezer bag.

Catalina Beef Stew

Prep. Time: about 15 minutes • Serves: 6 • Cost: about 63-cents per serving

2 lbs. stew beef, cut into cubes
1 bottle (8 oz) Catalina salad dressing
2 cups water
8-10 small potatoes, peeled and cubed
4-6 carrots, peeled and sliced
¼ cup oil
1½ teaspoons salt
½ teaspoon black pepper

In shallow dish, pour Catalina TM dressing over meat and set in refrigerator for at least 3 hours—preferably over night. Remove meat from marinade and drain. Pour marinade into slow cooker. In skillet heat oil and brown meat lightly on both sides. Drain meat. Combine meat, water, and vegetables in slow cooker. Add salt and pepper. Stir to blend well. Cover and cook on high for 5-6 hours or on low for 7-9 hours. Serve with biscuits.

WINTER STEW

Prep. Time: about 15 minutes • Serves: 6+ • Cost: about 49-cents per serving

2-3 lbs. stew beef, cubed
4-6 medium carrots, sliced
2-3 stalks celery, diced
8-10 medium potatoes, peeled and sliced
2 cans water chestnuts, drained and sliced, optional
2 medium onions, chopped
2 cans stewed tomatoes
2 cups beef broth
2 tablespoons flour
2 tablespoons sugar
2 teaspoons salt

Turn slow cooker on high. In small container, combine flour, sugar and salt. Pour beef broth into slow cooker and stir in flour mixture. Stir until flour mixture dissolves. Add all remaining ingredients. Cover with lid and cook on high for 5-6 hours or on low for 7-9 hours. Stir well before serving.

Oxtail Stew

Prep. Time: about 20 minutes • Serves: 8+ • Cost: about 72-cents per serving

2 lbs. beef stew meat, cut in small cubes

6 cups Oxtail Beef Stock (see page 95) or other quality beef broth

2 med. onions, chopped

½ to 1 teaspoon minced garlic, depending on taste

8-10 potatoes, cubed (this is especially good with new red potatoes
    with the skins left intact)

4 carrots, sliced

3 stalks celery, sliced or diced

2 med. turnips, peeled and chopped

1 teaspoon dried thyme

2 bay leaves

1 small can (4 oz.) tomato paste

1 teaspoon salt

½ teaspoon black pepper

½ teaspoon dried basil

Combine all ingredients in slow cooker. Cover with lid and cook on low
for 9-10 hours or on high for 6-7 hours. Remove bay leaves before serving.

Hungarian Stew

Prep. Time: about 20 minutes • Serves: 6 • Cost: about 55-cents per serving

1 medium head cabbage, shredded
1 lb. lean ground beef
1 lb. bulk sausage
OR use 2 lbs. bulk sausage instead of 1 lb. ground beef and 1 lb.
    sausage
¼ cup chopped green pepper
1 medium onion, chopped
1 teaspoon salt
½ teaspoon black pepper
1 can (24 oz.) tomato juice

Brown ground beef and sausage separately, drain off all fat, and crumble meat into slow cooker. Add all remaining ingredients, pouring tomato juice over all. Cover with lid and cook on high for 6 hours or on low for 8-9. Serve over cooked rice.

CHICKEN STEW WITH OKRA

Prep. Time: about 20 minutes • Serves: 6+ • Cost: about 67-cents per serving

1 whole chicken, cut in pieces, skin removed

2 large onions, chopped

2 green peppers, sliced

1 tablespoon salt

1 quart stewed tomatoes

1 pound fresh small okra, chopped

4 chicken bouillon cubes

4 cups water

2 cups uncooked instant rice

Combine all ingredients in slow cooker except the okra and rice. Cover with lid and cook on high for 5 hours. Remove meat from slow cooker and let cool. Remove chicken from bones and return meat to slow cooker. Add rice and chopped fresh okra. Cover with lid and reduce heat to low. Cook for an additional hour and then serve.

BRUNSWICK STEW

Prep. Time: about 20-25 minutes • Serves: 6+ • Cost: about 58-cents per serving

1 whole chicken fryer, skin removed, cut up

2 teaspoons salt

½ teaspoon black pepper

1 large onion, finely chopped

3 cups water

1 large can tomatoes with juice

1 cup sliced celery

½ cup barley

2 cans butter beans, drained

1 can whole kernel corn, drained

4 strips bacon, uncooked

2 tablespoons Worcestershire sauce

2 tablespoons butter

Put chicken in slow cooker with celery, onions, salt, pepper and water. Cover with lid and cook on high for 4 hours. Remove chicken and let cool. Add tomatoes, barley, corn, butter, beans, bacon, Worcestershire sauce and bacon slices cut up in small pieces. Remove chicken from bones and return pieces of meat to stew. Stir to blend well. Cover with lid and continue cooking on high for 4 additional hours.

CHICKEN ORIENTAL STEW

Prep. Time: about 10 minutes • Serves: 6+ • Cost: about 49-cents per serving

2 lbs. cooked chicken or turkey, cut in bite-sized pieces
6 cups chicken stock (see page 97)
3 stalks celery, chopped
1 can bean sprouts, drained
1 can bamboo shoots, drained
1 med. onion, chopped
1 (1 lb.) can Chinese mixed vegetables, drained
2 small cans water chestnuts, chopped and drained
¼ cup pimento pieces
½ to 1 lb. fresh mushrooms, sliced—optional
3 tablespoons cornstarch dissolved in½ cup cool water

Combine all ingredients in slow cooker. Cover with lid and cook on low for 8 hours or on high for 5 hours.

CHICKEN-POTATO STEW

Prep. Time: about 15 minutes • Serves: 6 • Cost: about 47-cents per serving

1 whole chicken, cut in pieces, skin removed
4 cups chicken stock (see page 97)
2 cups water
5 med. potatoes, peeled and cubed
2 large onions, chopped
3-4 carrots, sliced or diced
1 bag (10 oz.) fresh spinach, washed, trimmed
1½ cups milk
2 teaspoons salt
¼ teaspoon hot sauce
¼ to½ cup instant mashed potato flakes

Combine all ingredients in slow cooker except milk and instant mashed potatoes. Cover with lid and cook on low for 9 hours or on high for 6 hours. Remove chicken and let cool. Remove meat from bones and tear into pieces. Return meat to slow cooker. Add milk and instant potatoes. Stir to blend well. Allow stew to cook, uncovered, for another hour on low.

LAMB STEW

Prep. Time: 15 minutes • Serves: 6+ • Cost: about 73-cents per serving

3 lbs. lean lamb, cut in bite-sized chunks
2 medium onions, finely chopped
½ to 1 lb. fresh snow peas
1 can (20 oz.) stewed tomatoes
1 tablespoon honey
6-9 potatoes, peeled and cubed
1 teaspoon salt
½ teaspoon pepper
2 cups water
3 sprigs fresh parsley, chopped

Combine all ingredients in slow cooker. Cover with lid and cook on high for 4 hours. Reduce heat to low and continue cooking until you're ready to serve.

PORK 'N' HOMINY STEW

Prep. Time: about 15 minutes • Serves: 6+ • Cost: about 48-cents per serving

2 lbs. lean pork, cut into small pieces
2 large onions, chopped
2 tablespoons oil
2 garlic cloves, chopped
1 (1 lb.) can white hominy, drained
1 (1 lb.) can yellow hominy, drained
2 tablespoons chili powder
½ teaspoon ground cumin
2 tablespoons brown sugar
2 teaspoons salt, add more or less to taste
1 teaspoon dried oregano
½ teaspoon dried basil
6 medium-to-hot red chilies, seeds removed, chopped finely
Water

In skillet, heat oil and add garlic, chopped onion, and pork pieces. Cook until onion turns transparent, stirring and turning often. Transfer meat mixture to slow cooker. Add all remaining ingredients. Add enough water to cover contents. Cover with lid and cook on low for 9 hours or on high for 6 hours.

WEANIE-BEANIE STEW

Prep. Time: about 10 minutes • Serves: 6 • Cost: about 47-cents per serving

1 pkg. (1 lb.) pork hot dogs, cut in 1-inch pieces
4 cans pork 'n' beans
1 onion, chopped
1 cup chopped celery
½ cup chopped green bell pepper
¼ cup chili sauce
2 cups water
1 teaspoon salt
½ teaspoon pepper
2 cans cream of tomato soup, undiluted

Combine all ingredients in slow cooker. Cover with lid and cook on low for 7 hours.

Slow Cookers Have Multiple Uses

When you're not using your slow cooker for preparing wonderful food for your family, you can use it to add moisture to the atmosphere and to scent your home. To add moisture to the atmosphere, simply fill slow cooker three-quarters full and turn on low. Do not use the lid to cover the slow cooker. Allow the water to evaporate. This works great especially during the winter months. You can scent your entire home with a single slow cooker by adding liquid potpourri and letting it simmer on low without the lid. Another good way to add scent is to simmer cinnamon sticks, whole cloves, and other seasonings in water with the lid off. I've even added a few drops of fine perfume to water and let that simmer with no lid. When using your slow cooker for this, keep an eye on it that it doesn't go dry. And be sure to thoroughly clean the slow cooker before using it for cooking.

GREEN BEAN STEW

Prep. Time: about 15 minutes • Serves: 6+ • Cost: about 51-cents per serving

1 lb. stewing pork or beef, cubed
2 quarts green beans (fresh ones make this extra special in flavor!)
1 onion, finely chopped
1 small green pepper, finely chopped
1 cup chopped or thinly sliced celery
2 tablespoons butter
6 potatoes, cubed
1 quart canned or stewed tomatoes
2 teaspoons salt
½ teaspoon pepper
1 quart water

Place stewing pork or beef chunks in slow cooker. Add green beans. In a skillet, melt butter and saute onion and green pepper. Add celery and cook until onion is transparent. Pour vegetables and butter into slow cooker. Add potatoes, water, stewed tomatoes, salt and pepper. Cover with lid and cook on high for 6 hours or on low for 9 hours.

SPICY PORK STEW

Prep. Time: about 15 minutes • Serves: 6 • Cost: about 64-cents per serving

2 lbs. lean pork, cut into bite-sized pieces
2 tablespoons oil
¼ cup flour
1 clove garlic, minced
1 can (16 oz.) tomatoes, cut up with liquid
1 large onion, chopped
1 bay leaf
1 teaspoon sugar
2 teaspoons ham seasoning OR 2 beef bouillon cubes
½ teaspoon dried thyme
½ teaspoon dried oregano
¼ cup water
½ teaspoon salt
1 small green bell pepper, cut in thin strips
1 pkg. (10 oz.) frozen peas, thawed
6 small or 4 med. sweet potatoes, peeled and cubed

In skillet, heat oil and add onion, garlic, and pork. Cook until onion turns transparent, stirring often and browning the meat on all sides. Remove meat and vegetables from skillet and drain. In reserved oil, stir in flour to form a paste. Add tomatoes with their liquid,¼ cup water, and½ teaspoon salt. Pour skillet mixture into slow cooker. Add all remaining ingredients. Cover with lid and cook on low for 9 hours or on high for 6 hours. Remove bay leaf before serving.

V-8® STEW

Prep. Time: about 10 minutes • Serves: 6 • Cost: about 41-cents per serving

2 lbs. lean pork, cut in small pieces
1 med. onion, chopped
1 qt. V-8 juice®
5 potatoes, peeled and cubed
2 pkgs. (10 oz.) frozen mixed vegetables, thawed
Salt and pepper to taste

Combine all ingredients in slow cooker. Cover with lid and cook on low for 8 hours or on high for 5 hours.

VENISON PINTO STEW

Prep. Time: about 15 minutes • Serves: 6 • Cost: about 47-cents per serving

2 lbs. venison, cut into small pieces
1½ cups dry pinto beans
Water
½ teaspoon baking soda
½ teaspoon salt
2 med. onions, chopped
2 cups frozen corn, thawed and drained
2 tablespoons cornstarch dissolved in½ cup cool water
2 stalks celery, diced
1 teaspoon salt
6 cups beef broth

Soak pinto beans in water overnight. The next morning, drain beans and put in saucepan. Cover with fresh water and½ teaspoon salt. Bring beans to a rapid boil and let cook for about 5 minutes. Transfer pan to sink and add 1 teaspoon baking soda to beans. This will cause the beans to foam. Rinse beans twice, draining each time in a colander. Transfer beans to slow cooker. Add all remaining ingredients. Cover with lid and cook on low for 9 hours or on high for 6 hours.

Hearty Venison Stew

Prep. Time: about 15 minutes • Serves: 8 • Cost: about 49-cents per serving

2 lbs. venison, cut into small pieces
8-10 potatoes, peeled and cubed
3 large carrots, sliced
1 large onion, chopped
2 tablespoons butter or margarine
2 cups green beans
½ cup pearl barley
1 cup sweet corn
1 cup peas
1 teaspoon salt
½ teaspoon pepper

In skillet, melt butter or margarine and saute onion until transparent. Transfer onions to slow cooker. Add all remaining ingredients. Cover with lid and cook on low for 9 hours or on high for 6 hours.

When Cooking Ahead...

If I know a busy week is approaching, often I will cook ahead in preparation for that tight schedule. That way, dinner is waiting in the freezer and the kids can simply remove the container, thaw, heat, and serve. When using my slow cookers for cooking ahead, here are some things I've learned the hard way:

• Save potatoes from the freezer. When I've frozen stews with potatoes or casseroles that have been cooked in a slow cooker, I've discovered the potatoes get rubbery and like to crumble. So I withhold potatoes until after I've thawed the dish and I cook them, then add the potatoes when I'm ready to serve the meal.

• Hold off adding pasta to slow cooker dishes if you intend to freeze the contents and serve them later. Pasta is best when prepared fresh for the meal you wish to serve.

• Cream-based soups will separate when frozen. I haven't been able to re-warm a cream-based soup and have it the same consistency as when I first cooked it. So my recommendation is don't prepare a cream-based soup for the freezer.

SECTION III

Chowders

I tried to find a definition of what makes a chowder different than a soup or stew and couldn't really find anything other than most chowders have a milk or cream base. But not always. I've included one recipe that has a tomato-base. If you're a fan of creamy chowders, I'm sure you'll enjoy these recipes. They're so good when served with fresh homemade bread or rolls.

Garden Chowder

Prep. Time: about 20 minutes • Servings: 8+ • Cost: about 55-cents per serving

2 cups chopped celery

2 cups fresh corn, cut off the cob, OR 3 cans corn, drained

1 or 2 fresh onions, chopped

1 small green or red sweet pepper, chopped

6 meaty tomatoes, skins removed and chopped, or 1 large can
   stewed tomatoes with juice

3 cups water

8-10 potatoes, peeled and cubed

1 teaspoon salt, add more or less according to taste

½ teaspoon seasoned salt

¼ to½ teaspoon black pepper

1 teaspoon garlic powder

2 teaspoons parsley flakes

2 teaspoons basil

4 tablespoons butter

3 tablespoons flour

2 cups milk

2 cups shredded cheddar cheese

½ teaspoon paprika

In slow cooker, combine celery, corn, onion, sweet pepper, tomatoes, potatoes, salt, seasoned salt, pepper and 3 cups water. Cook on high for 6 hours. In saucepan, melt butter and stir in flour to make a paste. Gradually add milk, stirring constantly. Increase heat to medium and continue stirring until mixture forms a gravy-like sauce. Add paprika to sauce. Pour sauce into slow cooker over vegetables. Cover with lid and cook on low for 2 hours longer. Serve with shredded cheddar cheese sprinkled over each serving.

Broccoli Chowder

Prep. Time: about 15 minutes • Serves: 6 • Cost: about 34-cents per serving

1 lb. fresh broccoli, chopped
1 onion, chopped
½ lb. bacon
2 stalks celery, diced
5 med. potatoes, cubed
2 carrots, sliced or diced
1 cup water
1 teaspoon salt
½ teaspoon pepper
1 teaspoon dillweed
2 tablespoons cornstarch dissolved in½ cup water
1 quart milk
2 cups shredded or grated Cheddar cheese

In skillet, fry bacon until crisp. Remove from grease and drain; set bacon aside. In remaining bacon grease, saute onion, celery, and potatoes until onion turns transparent.. Transfer all vegetables from skillet to slow cooker. Add chopped broccoli, carrots, seasonings, and 1 cup water. Cover with lid and cook on low for 6 hours. Add milk, cheese, and cornstarch water. Stir to blend well. Cover with lid and continue cooking for another 1-2 hours. Crumble bacon over each serving.

CREOLE BEAN CHOWDER

Prep. Time: about 10 minutes • Serves: 6 • Cost: about 41-cents per serving

2 cups navy beans, soaked in water overnight
1 smoked ham-hock
2 cups shredded carrots
2 med. onions, chopped
2 stalks celery, chopped
2 cups chopped okra
¼ cup finely chopped green bell pepper
¼ cup finely chopped red bell pepper
2 cups stewed tomatoes with juice
2 cans cream of tomato soup
1 teaspoon salt
½ teaspoon pepper

Set ham-hock in center of slow cooker. Add all remaining ingredients, except salt and pepper, around and over ham-hock. Cover with lid and cook on low for 9 hours. Add salt and pepper when ready to serve. Remove ham-hock before serving.

CHEESY CHOWDER

Prep. Time: about 15 minutes • Serves: 6 • Cost: about 41-cents per serving

3 med. potatoes, cubed
2 carrots, diced or sliced
1 stalk celery, diced
½ cup finely chopped green bell pepper
4 tablespoons butter or margarine
3 cups chicken broth
2 cups half and half
½ cup flour
3 cups shredded sharp American or Cheddar cheese
1 tablespoon fresh parsley, chopped fine

Combine potatoes, carrots, celery, green pepper, and chicken broth in slow cooker. Cover with lid and cook on low for 6 hours. In saucepan, melt butter and stir in flour to form a paste. Quickly add half and half and continue stirring this mixture over a medium heat until it thickens. When it begins to thicken, add cheese and continue stirring until cheese melts. Pour cheese mixture into slow cooker. Add salt and season according to your tastes. Garnish each serving with freshly chopped parsley.

Ham Chowder

Prep. Time: about 20 minutes • Servings: 8+ • Cost: about 67-cents per serving

2 cups (or more) diced ham
1 large sweet onion, diced
8-10 potatoes, peeled and diced
2 cups water
1 quart milk
2 cans creamed corn
1 can sweet corn, drained
1 smoked ham-hock
1 teaspoon salt
¼ teaspoon pepper
1 teaspoon parsley flakes
½ teaspoon sweet basil
¼ teaspoon thyme
2 tablespoons cornstarch dissolved in½ cup cool water

Combine all ingredients in slow cooker. Cover with lid and cook on high for 5 hours or on low for 8-9 hours. Remove ham-hock before serving.

HAM AND CHEESE CHOWDER

Prep. Time: about 20 minutes • Servings: 8+ • Cost: about 64-cents per serving

3 cups water

8-10 medium potatoes, diced

2 cups ham, cubed

2 stalks celery, diced

3-5 carrots, sliced

1 large onion, chopped

2 teaspoons salt

½ teaspoon black pepper

1-2 lbs. American cheese, cubed

½ cup parmesan cheese

¼ cup butter

¼ cup flour

2 cups milk

Combine potatoes, onions, celery, carrots and ham in slow cooker. Pour water over vegetables. Add salt and pepper. Cover with lid and cook on high for 5 hours. In saucepan, melt butter and stir in flour to form a paste. Add 2 cups milk and continue heating over medium-high heat; stirring constantly until mixture thickens. Add parmesan and American cheese to white sauce and stir until dissolved. Pour cheese sauce over vegetables and ham in slow cooker. Stir to blend well. This can be kept warm by reducing the heat setting to low until you're ready to serve.

German Sausage Chowder

Prep. Time: about 5 minutes • Serves: 8 • Cost: about 52-cents per serving

2 lbs. cooked bratwurst or knackwurst, cut into ½-inch slices
6-8 med. potatoes, peeled and cubed
1 onion, chopped
6 cups shredded cabbage
1 qt.. half and half
2 tablespoons cornstarch dissolved in ½ cup cool water
1 lb. Swiss cheese, grated or chopped
1 teaspoon dried parsley
2 cups water

Combine all ingredients in slow cooker except half and half, the cornstarch water, and cheese. Cover with lid and cook on low for 8 hours. Add half and half, cornstarch water, and cheese. Stir to blend well. Continue cooking, uncovered, for another hour then serve.

Don't Use A Slow Cooker On Your Stove Top

I've learned many things by trial and error. And one major error I learned the hard way was to set my removable slow cooker directly on the heating element of my electric range. One of my kids had used the burner to heat water in the tea kettle and when they flipped the dial to turn it off, they failed to turn it all the way off. As a result, the burner was on low and I didn't realize it. I was doing dishes and just happened to set the empty slow cooker on the stove top after cleaning off the table. Within just a few minutes I heard a loud pop! My precious slow cooker cracked completely in two. And broken slow cookers can't be glued back together!

BASIC CORN CHOWDER

Prep. Time: about 15 minutes • Serves: 10+ • Cost: about 37-cents per serving

1 lb. bacon
1 large onion, chopped
3-4 stalks celery, chopped
3-4 med. carrots, chopped
5-8 med. potatoes, peeled and cubed
3 cans creamed corn
2 quarts half and half
¼ to ½ cup instant mashed potato flakes
1 teaspoon salt
½ teaspoon pepper
6 cups water

In skillet cook bacon until crisp, drain and set aside. In remaining bacon grease, cook onion, celery, and potatoes until onion turns transparent. Drain vegetables then add to slow cooker. Add carrots, creamed corn, salt, pepper, and water. Cover with lid and cook on low for 7 hours. Add half and half and potato flakes and stir to blend well. Leave uncovered and continue cooking for another hour. Crumble crisp bacon over chowder and stir well before serving.

CREAMY CORN CHOWDER WITH SAUSAGE

Prep. Time: about 15 minutes • Servings: 6+ • Cost: about 68-cents per serving

2 lbs. smoked sausage, cut into thin round slices
½ lb. bacon
¼ cup flour
2 medium onions, chopped finely
3 cups water
4 chicken bouillon cubes
3 cans creamed-style corn
2 cans whole kernel sweet corn with juice
6-9 potatoes, peeled and cubed
1/8 teaspoon white pepper
3 drops red pepper sauce
2 cups half and half
2 tablespoons butter or margarine

In skillet, fry bacon until crisp. Remove bacon and let drain on either paper toweling or brown paper. In remaining bacon grease, cook chopped onions until they turn transparent. Add sausage slices and lightly brown. Drain off grease from sausage and onions. Transfer to slow cooker. Add 2 cups water, potatoes, creamed corn, white pepper and pepper sauce to slow cooker. Cover with lid and cook on low for 7-8 hours. In skillet melt butter or margarine. Stir in flour to form a paste, then quickly add half and half. Dissolve bouillon cubes in remaining cup of water and add that to skillet. Keep stirring until mixture thickens into a gravy. Pour gravy into slow cooker. Stir to blend well. Cover with lid and allow flavors to blend for about an hour. Crumble crisp bacon over each serving.

WHITE CORN CHOWDER

Prep. Time: about 20 minutes • Servings: 8+ • Cost: about 63-cents per serving

½ lb. bacon
1 onion, finely chopped
8-10 potatoes, peeled and diced
1 stalk celery, sliced
2 carrots, diced
2 cups milk
2 cups water, boiling
4 chicken bouillon cubes
3 cans white corn, drained
1 teaspoon salt
½ teaspoon pepper
2 tablespoons cornstarch dissolved in½ cup cool water

In skillet, fry bacon until crisp and drain. Measure¼ cup bacon drippings and discard remaining grease. Pour¼ cup bacon grease back in skillet. Saute onion, celery, and potatoes in hot grease, stirring often until vegetables are lightly browned. Pour vegetables into slow cooker. Add diced carrots. Dissolve chicken bouillon in hot water and pour into slow cooker. Add milk, corn, salt and pepper. Stir to mix well. Cover with lid and cook on high for 5 hours. In separate container, dissolve cornstarch in cold water. Pour into slow cooker and stir. Crumble crisp bacon and add to the slow cooker. Cover again, reduce heat to low, and continue cooking for 2-3 hours.

Hearty Corn Chowder

Prep. Time: about 20 minutes • Servings: 6+ • Cost: about 58-cents per serving

2 cans creamed-style sweet corn
1 can whole-kernel sweet corn, drained
2 cups milk
3 tablespoons butter or margarine
1 medium onion, finely chopped
2 cups finely diced ham
5-8 potatoes, peeled and cubed
½ cup water
1 teaspoon salt
½ teaspoon black pepper

In small skillet, melt butter and saute chopped onion until transparent. Pour butter and onion in slow cooker. Add all remaining ingredients except the milk. Stir to blend well. Cover with lid and cook on low for 6 hours. Add milk and stir to blend well. Let chowder cook for an additional hour then ladle into soup bowls. Serve with crusty rolls.

CORN DOGGIE CHOWDER

Prep. Time: about 20 minutes • Servings: 8+ • Cost: about 72-cents per serving

2 quarts milk
8-10 white potatoes, peeled and cubed
2 large onions, chopped
2 stalks celery, chopped
3 cans creamed-style sweet corn
8 slices bacon
1 teaspoon salt
½ to 1 teaspoon black pepper, depending upon taste
½ teaspoon celery salt
2 lbs. or about 16 hot dogs, sliced
2 tablespoons cornstarch dissolved in½ cup cool water

In skillet over medium heat, cook bacon until crisp. Remove bacon and drain. In hot grease, saute onions until transparent. Drain and then transfer onions to slow cooker. Add potatoes, celery, corn, salt, pepper, and celery salt to slow cooker. Cover with lid and cook on low for 6 hours. Add milk, cornstarch water and hot dog slices. Return cover to slow cooker and continue cooking for 2 hours longer.

SHORTCUT CLAM CHOWDER

Prep. Time: about 15 minutes • Servings: 6+ • Cost: about 72-cents per serving

2 cans clams
2 cans creamed corn
2 tablespoons butter or margarine
1 onion, finely chopped
1 can cream of potato soup
2 cans Campbell's™ Clam Chowder (no tomatoes)
Milk, beginning with 1 cup at a time

In skillet, melt butter and saute onion until it is transparent. Add all cans of soup; stir to blend well. Pour into slow cooker. Add creamed corn to slow cooker. Add one cup of milk and stir. Add more milk to get desired consistency. Cover with lid and cook on low for 6 hours or longer. Rinse clams with a little water, then add to slow cookerduring the last hour of cooking.

 Keep Your Slow Cooker in the Clear

I don't know how it is in your house, but my kitchen is not large enough to allow me all the room I need. As a result, it's not uncommon for paper, pens, crayons, markers, books, etc. to accumulate next to where I store my slow cookers on the counter. One of my slow cookers is kept at the end of the counter, up against the kitchen wall. Without even thinking, I filled my slow cooker and turned it on without pulling it out from next to the wall. Somehow one of my daughter's crayons and a piece of paper was wedged under the slow cooker towards the back where I couldn't readily see it. What happened is the crayon melted and the paper turned brown and started to singe. The awful odor of the melting crayon and singing paper led me to the source, fortunately, before a fire broke out. So please take a lesson from my experience—always pull out the slow cooker and check to make sure nothing is under it or leaning against it before you plug it in and start cooking with it.

FISH CHOWDER

Prep. Time: about 15 minutes • Serves: 8 • Cost: about 62-cents per serving

3 lbs. fresh or frozen fish fillets, thawed
6 med. potatoes, peeled and cubed
1 onion, chopped
1 stalk celery, chopped
2 carrots, diced
1 can cream-styled corn
4 cups fish stock (see page 103)
½ lb. bacon
¼ cup flour
2 cups milk
½ teaspoon dried thyme
1 teaspoon salt
½ teaspoon pepper

Combine potatoes, carrot, creamed corn, and fish stock in slow cooker. Cover with lid and cook on low for 4 hours. After 4 hours of cooking time, cook bacon in skillet until crisp. Drain bacon and set aside. Empty skillet of all grease, then return 4 tablespoons grease. In bacon grease, saute onion and celery until onion turns transparent. Add flour and stir to form a paste. Gradually add milk and continue stirring until mixture thickens and forms a gravy. Pour into slow cooker. Cut fish fillets into 2-inch chunks and add them to the slow cooker. Add all remaining ingredients, except the bacon. Cover with lid and continue cooking on low for 2 hours. Stir before serving. Crumble crisp bacon generously over each serving.

Chicken 'n' Veggie Chowder

Prep. Time: about 15 minutes • Servings: 6+ • Cost: about 72-cents per serving

2 cans evaporated milk
3 teaspoons chicken bouillon or seasoning mix
2-3 tablespoons butter or margarine
1 heaping tablespoon cornstarch dissolved in 1 cup cool water
2 cups milk
2 lbs. American cheese, cubed
1 pkg. (10 oz.) frozen sweet corn, thawed and drained
2 cans creamed-style corn
1 bag (10 oz) frozen broccoli, thawed and drained
2 teaspoons salt
½ teaspoon pepper
1 small onion, finely chopped
1 teaspoon parsley flakes
1 teaspoon sweet basil
4 pieces boneless, skinless chicken breast fillets

In skillet melt butter or margarine and saute onion for about 3 minutes. Stir in chicken seasoning. Add both cans evaporated milk and cornstarch water. Continue to cook and stir mixture until it thickens and becomes a thick gravy consistency. Pour mixture into slow cooker. Add all remaining ingredients reserving the chicken for last. Cover with lid and cook on low for 6-8 hours. When ready to serve, remove all pieces of chicken; cube them and return chicken to the chowder. Stir to blend well then ladle chowder into serving bowls.

PENNY'S CHICKEN CORN CHOWDER

Prep. Time: about 20 minutes • Servings: 8+ • Cost: about 72-cents per serving

2 cans evaporated milk
2 teaspoons chicken bouillon or seasoning mix
1 tablespoon cornstarch dissolved in½ cup water
2 tablespoons butter or margarine
2 cups milk
2 lbs. American cheese, cubed
1 pkg. frozen sweet corn, thawed and drained
2 teaspoons salt
½ teaspoon pepper
1 tablespoon minced dried onions
1 teaspoon parsley flakes
1 teaspoon sweet basil
4 pieces boneless, skinless chicken breast fillets

In skillet melt butter or margarine and stir in chicken bouillon or seasoning mix. Add both cans evaporated milk and cornstarch water. Cook over medium heat, stirring constantly, until mixture thickens to a gravy consistency. Pour mixture into slow cooker while near boiling hot. Add milk and onion; stir to mix well. Add all spices and cheese. Turn slow cooker on high. Drop in corn. Arrange chicken fillets on top. Cover with lid and cook for 6-7 hours. When ready to serve, remove all pieces of chicken; cube them and return chicken to the chowder. Stir to blend well then ladle chowder into serving bowls.

Smokey Buttons & Potato Chowder

Prep. Time: about 15 minutes • Servings: 8+ • Cost: about 65-cents per serving

2 boxes dehydrated scalloped potatoes (any brand name)
2 lbs. smoked sausage links, cut in ½-inch "buttons"
1 large or 2 small onions, diced
3 cups water
2 tablespoons cornstarch
4 cups milk
¼ cup butter or margarine
Salt and pepper to taste

In skillet melt butter or margarine and saute onion until transparent. Pour onion-butter into slow cooker. Add powdered mix from scalloped potato mixes and 2 cups water. Stir until powder is dissolved. Add dehydrated potatoes, sausage, and the milk. Stir to mix well. Cover with lid and cook on low for 6 hours. Dissolve cornstarch in remaining 2 cups water and add to slow cooker. Stir to blend well. Return lid to slow cooker and continue cooking for another 2 hours.

Hearty Potato Chowder

Prep. Time: about 10 minutes • Serves: 8+ • Cost: about 33-cents per serving

8-10 medium potatoes, cubed
5 carrots, sliced or diced
6 stalks celery, sliced or diced
2 onions, chopped
1 quart milk
2 cups water
2 teaspoons salt
¾ teaspoon black pepper
3 tablespoons cornstarch dissolved in ½ cup cool water
2 tablespoons butter or margarine

Prepare potatoes and put them in slow cooker. Add carrots, celery, 2 cups water, salt and pepper. Cover with lid and cook on low for 7 hours. Dissolve cornstarch in ½ cup cold water. In skillet, melt butter or margarine and saute onion until transparent. Add milk and cornstarch water, stir constantly over medium-high heat until mixture begins to boil and thicken. Pour into slow cooker. Stir before serving.

German Spud Chowder

Prep. Time: about 20 minutes • Serves: 5+ • Cost: about 35-cents per serving

4 to 6 slices bacon
1 onion, chopped
3 carrots, chopped
2 stalks celery, chopped
¼ cup flour
3 cups beef broth
2 cups milk
2 beef bouillon cubes
10 medium potatoes, peeled and chopped

In skillet, fry bacon until crisp. Remove bacon and drain while browning onion, carrot and celery in hot grease. Remove vegetables from grease and drain. Add flour to hot grease and stir to form a paste. Add milk to skillet and continue stirring until mixture begins to thicken. Pour gravy mixture into slow cooker. Add potatoes, vegetables, beef broth, and beef bouillon cubes. Stir to blend well. Cover with lid and cook on low for 7 hours.

CHAPTER IV

Stocks

Getting vegetables into my picky eaters hasn't always been easy. That is, until I learned how to hide vegetables in soup stocks and sauces. The following stock recipes are very versatile and can be used in a variety of dishes. Generally, they're very inexpensive because you make stock from the leftover carcasses or bones from meat that you serve at other meals. Save whatever stock you don't use by freezing or canning. This will help keep your grocery expenses down, give you added convenience of already having it on hand, and provide your family with a nutrient-rich homemade stock that tastes better than any store-brand variety can offer! If you decide not to freeze or can your stock, be sure to use it within a few days before it goes bad. Always store stock in covered containers in the refridgerator.

BEEFY MUSHROOM STOCK WITH HIDDEN VEGETABLES

Prep. Time: about 10 minutes • Cost: about 12-cents per serving

3-4 cups water
2 tablespoon beef bouillon
1-2 whole onions, peeled and quartered
1-2 stalks of celery, cleaned and cut in chunks
1 tablespoon Worcestershire sauce™
1 can of cream of mushroom soup
2 teaspoons salt
½ teaspoon black pepper
Several fresh, cleaned mushrooms
1 teaspoon minced garlic—optional
Optional vegetables: zucchini; yellow summer squash, or leaks

Mix water, soup and bouillon together first then add the rest of the ingredients to slow cooker. Cover with lid and cook on high for at least 4 hours. Let contents cool and then puree 1-2 cups at a time in the blender, each time placing puree back in the slow cooker. This stock may be placed in freezer containers or processed in pint/quart canning jars so that it is handy on the shelf for use with other recipes.

Oxtail Beef Stock

Prep. Time: about 10 minutes • Cost: about 11-cents per serving

1-2 meaty oxtail bones or other beef bones
8 cups water
2 onions, quartered
2 stalks celery, chopped
1 clove garlic, peeled
2 teaspoons beef bouillon powder
2-3 teaspoons salt, depending upon taste
½ to 1 teaspoon black pepper, depending upon taste
2 tablespoons Worcestershire sauce™

Combine all ingredients in slow cooker. Cover with lid and cook on low for 9 hours. Remove vegetables and put them in blender. Add 1 cup water to vegetables and puree. Remove bones and discard (or give them to your dog!). Pour stock through a sieve or strainer. Add pureed vegetables to clear broth. Pour broth in large bowl or several wide-mouth jars and store overnight in refrigerator. Fat will congeal and form a crust on top. Remove fat crust and reheat stock. Pour into ice-cube freezer trays and freeze, then store frozen cubes in a freezer bag. Or this stock can be put in freezer containers or in pint/ quart canning jars and processed for future use.

GINGER BEEF STOCK

Prep. Time: about 10 minutes • Cost: about 14-cents per serving

3-4 lbs. beef stewing bones with marrow
2 med. onions, quartered
1 large carrot, cut into thirds
3 slices fresh ginger, about ¼-inch thick
2 whole cloves
2 bay leaves
1½ teaspoons salt
10 peppercorns
8 cups water

Combine all ingredients in slow cooker. Cover with lid and cook on low for 7 hours. Remove lid and skim scum off top. Increase heat to high and continue cooking without the lid for 2-3 hours. Pour slow cooker contents through colander or sieve. Discard bones (or give them to your dog), vegetables, and seasonings. Set clear broth in refrigerator overnight. Fat will separate and form a white crust at the top. Remove fat and discard. Broth will become gel-like as it chills. Freeze in a covered container or use immediately.

BASIC CHICKEN STOCK

Prep. Time: about 10 minutes • Cost: about 10-cents per serving

carcass of 1 chicken, including neck, bones and skin
2 onions, quartered
3 stalks celery, chopped
1-2 cloves garlic, peeled
8 cups water
2 teaspoons salt
½ teaspoon black pepper
1 bay leaf
2 teaspoons chicken bouillon granules or 2 cubes chicken bouillon

Combine all ingredients in slow cooker. Cover with lid and cook on low for 8 hours. Pour stock through a sieve or strainer. Discard bones, skin, and bay leaf. Remove vegetables and put in blender. Add 1 cup liquid and puree vegetables. Add pureed vegetables to clear broth. Pour broth in large bowl or several wide-mouth jars and refrigerate overnight. The fat will separate and form a crust on the top. Remove fat and discard. Reheat broth and pour into ice-cube freezer trays and freeze, then store frozen cubes in a freezer bag. Or this stock can be put in freezer containers or in pint/quart canning jars and processed for future use.

PICKY EATER'S CHICKEN STOCK

Prep. Time: about 10 minutes • Cost: about 12-cents per serving

Author's Note: If you enjoy a rich, full-bodied broth for your chicken noodle or rice soup, then you'll love this stock recipe. I've even used this for making chicken pot pie, various casseroles, and the famous dish of "Arroz con Pollo." Don't be afraid to put this recipe to the test with your picky eaters. I'm sure it will pass without anyone suspecting there's any vegetables in it at all.

1-2 chicken carcasses, including bones and skin, in pieces
6 cups water
2-4 stalks of celery, cut into chunks
1 carrot, cut up
1 whole onion, peeled and quartered
2 teaspoons salt
½ teaspoon black pepper
1 tablespoon poultry seasoning
Add any vegetable that will puree without adding color such as
     summer squash, peeled zucchini, leeks, etc.

Combine all ingredients in slow cooker. Cover with lid and cook on low for 7-9 hours. Pour contents through colander or sieve; discard bones and skin. Pick out cooked vegetables and puree them in a blender with a cup of broth. Add puree back to broth. Pour broth in large bowl or several wide-mouth jars and refrigerate overnight. The fat will separate and form a crust on the top. Remove fat and discard. Reheat broth and pour into ice-cube freezer trays and freeze, then store frozen cubes in a freezer bag. Or this stock can be put in freezer containers or in pint/quart canning jars and processed for future use.

CREAMY VEGETABLE CHICKEN STOCK

Prep. Time: about 10 minutes • Cost: about 14-cents per serving

1-2 chicken carcasses, including bones and skin, in pieces
6 cups water
2 cans of cream of chicken soup
1 can of cream of celery soup
1 whole onion, peeled and quartered
2 teaspoons salt
½ teaspoon black pepper
1 yellow summer squash or peeled zucchini—optional
2 teaspoons poultry seasoning or 1 tablespoon of chicken bouillon
Add any vegetable that will puree without adding color such as
     summer squash, peeled zucchini, leeks, etc.

Combine all ingredients in slow cooker. Cover with lid and cook on low for 7-9 hours. Pour contents through colander or sieve; discard bones and skin. Pick out cooked vegetables and puree them in a blender with a cup of broth. Add puree back to broth. Pour broth in large bowl or several wide-mouth jars and refrigerate overnight. The fat will separate and form a crust on the top. Remove fat and discard. Reheat broth and pour into ice-cube freezer trays and freeze, then store frozen cubes in a freezer bag. Or this stock can be put in freezer containers or in pint/quart canning jars and processed for future use.

DELUXE CHICKEN STOCK

Prep. Time: about 15 minutes • *Cost: about 13-cents*
per serving

2 whole chicken carcasses, including bones and skin, in pieces
8 cups water
2 medium onions, 1 quartered and 1 chopped
2 tablespoons butter or margarine
3 stalks celery, cut in thirds
1 carrot, cut in small chunks
1 teaspoon salt
½ teaspoon dried thyme
2 bay leaves

Break chicken carcasses in pieces and place in slow cooker. Add water, the quartered onion, celery, and carrot. In skillet or saucepan, melt butter or margarine and saute chopped onion until onion turns transparent. Pour cooked onion and butter in slow cooker over carcasses. Sprinkle 1 teaspoon salt over contents. Add thyme and bay leaves. Cover with lid and cook on low for 7-9 hours. After cooking, pour contents through colander or sieve; discard bones and skin. Pick out cooked vegetables and puree them in a blender with a cup of broth. Add puree back to broth. Pour broth in large bowl or several wide-mouth jars and refrigerate overnight. The fat will separate and form a crust on the top. Remove fat and discard. Reheat broth and pour into ice-cube freezer trays and freeze, then store frozen cubes in a freezer bag. Or this stock can be put in freezer containers or in pint/quart canning jars and processed for future use.

DUCK STOCK

Prep. Time: about 15 minutes • Cost: about 16-cents per serving

1 duck carcass, including bones and skin, cut into pieces
1 small onion, quartered
1 med. carrot, cut into chunks
1 stalk celery, cut into thirds
1 small tomato, coarsely chopped
1 cup fresh mushrooms, minced
1 clove garlic, minced
1 teaspoon dried parsley flakes
1 bay leaf
6-8 cups water
1 teaspoon salt
½ teaspoon pepper

Combine all ingredients in slow cooker and cover with water. Cover with lid and cook on low for 9 hours. Pour contents through colander or sieve; discard bones and skin. Pick out cooked vegetables and puree them in a blender with a cup of broth. Add puree back to broth. Pour broth in large bowl or several wide-mouth jars and refrigerate overnight. The fat will separate and form a crust on the top. Remove fat and discard. Reheat broth and pour into ice-cube freezer trays and freeze, then store frozen cubes in a freezer bag. Or this stock can be put in freezer containers or in pint/quart canning jars and processed for future use.

TURKEY STOCK

Prep. Time: about 10 minutes • Cost: about 10-cents per serving

1 turkey carcass, including bones and skin, cut into pieces
2 onions, quartered
2 stalks celery, cut in thirds
6 cups water
1 teaspoon salt (or more to taste)
½ teaspoon black pepper
1 teaspoon poultry seasoning or 2 teaspoons chicken bouillon

Combine all ingredients in slow cooker. Cover with lid and cook on low for 9 hours. Remove bones and discard. Spoon vegetables out and put them in a blender. Pour broth through a sieve or strainer. Add 1 cup clear broth to blender and puree vegetables. Return pureed broth to clear broth. Stir to blend well. Pour into ice-cube freezer trays and freeze, then store frozen cubes in a freezer bag. Or this stock can be put in freezer containers or in pint/quart canning jars and processed for future use.

BASIC FISH STOCK

Prep. Time: about 15 minutes • Cost: about 13-cents per serving

About 3 lbs. fresh fish, cleaned with entrails removed, bones left
    intact
1 onion, quartered
1 carrot, chopped
2 stalks celery, chopped
2-3 teaspoons salt
½ teaspoon black pepper
1 teaspoon dried parsley
8 cups water

Tie fish up in a large piece of cheesecloth. Combine all ingredients in slow cooker, setting fish in center. Cover with lid and cook on low for 6 hours. Remove slow cooker from heat source and let cool. Discard fish. When vegetables are cool, begin by pureeing 1 to 2 cups vegetables with broth, in blender. Return pureed mixture to slow cooker. Continue using the blender until all vegetables have been pureed. Stir to blend well. Pour into ice-cube freezer trays and freeze, then store frozen cubes in a freezer bag. Or this stock can be put in freezer containers or in pint/quart canning jars and processed for future use.

HAM STOCK

Prep. Time: about 5 minutes • Cost: about 10-cents per serving

2 smoked ham-hocks
8 cups water
2 onions, quartered
2 stalks celery, chopped
1 teaspoon salt
½ teaspoon black pepper

Combine all ingredients in slow cooker. Cover with lid and cook on low for 7-9 hours. Remove bones and discard. Spoon vegetables out and put them in a blender. Pour broth through a sieve or strainer. Add 1 cup clear broth to blender and puree vegetables. Return pureed broth to clear broth. Stir to blend well. Pour into ice-cube freezer trays and freeze, then store frozen cubes in a freezer bag. Or this stock can be put in freezer containers or in pint/quart canning jars and processed for future use.

 Recipe Shortcut

If you're not in a hurry to get your meal put together and cooking, you can sauté onion, celery, garlic, or mushrooms in your slow cooker. Simply add the butter or margarine to the bottom of the slow cooker. Add vegetables. Turn slow cooker on high and let the butter melt and the vegetables cook uncovered while you work on something else. Since I'm famous for "multi-tasking" this works for me when I'm trying to coordinate and juggle several tasks at the same time. After about an hour, I add the remaining ingredients to the slow cooker and then go on to something else while the slow cooker does its thing.

BASIC VEGETABLE STOCK

Prep. Time: about 10 minutes • Cost: about 13-cents per serving

1 quart tomato juice
½ green pepper, seeds removed, chopped
3 stalks celery, chopped
2 onions, quartered
1 lb. zucchini and/or yellow summer squash, cubed
8 cups water
1-2 cloves garlic, peeled
2 teaspoons salt
½ teaspoon black pepper
½ teaspoon seasoned salt

Combine all ingredients in slow cooker. Cover with lid and cook on low for 6-8 hours. Remove slow cooker from heat source and let cool. When vegetables are cool, begin by pureeing 1 to 2 cups vegetables with broth, in blender. Return pureed mixture to slow cooker. Continue using the blender until all vegetables have been pureed. Stir to blend well. Pour into ice-cube freezer trays and freeze, then store frozen cubes in a freezer bag. Or this stock can be put in freezer containers or in pint/quart canning jars and processed for future use.

CLEAR VEGETABLE STOCK

Prep. Time: about 15 minutes • Cost: about 12-cents per serving

2 large onions, quartered
2 leeks, chopped
4 stalks celery, chopped
2 cloves garlic, peeled
1 lb. zucchini, peeled and chopped
1 lb. yellow summer squash, peeled and chopped
8 cups water
2 teaspoons chicken bouillon mix, optional
2 teaspoons salt
½ teaspoon black pepper
½ teaspoon seasoned salt

Chop vegetables and tie up in a large piece of cheesecloth. Drop cheesecloth in slow cooker and add water and bouillon, salt, pepper and seasoned salt. Cover with lid and cook on low for 8 hours. Remove slow cooker from heat source and let cool. Remove cheesecloth with vegetables and either discard or use them in another dish. Pour into ice-cube freezer trays and freeze, then store frozen cubes in a freezer bag. Or this stock can be put in freezer containers or in pint/quart canning jars and processed for future use.

TOMATO-BASED STOCK

Prep. Time: about 25 minutes • Cost: about 14-cents per serving

10-15 medium to large tomatoes
2 cloves garlic, peeled
2 large onions, quartered
4 stalks celery, chopped
½ green pepper, chopped
8 cups water
2 teaspoons dried basil
½ teaspoon dried oregano
1 bay leaf
2 teaspoons salt
½ teaspoon black pepper

In large pan, bring about 2 quarts of water to a fast boil. Drop tomatoes in boiling water, 2 or 3 at a time and let cook for 30-45 seconds. Remove tomatoes and immerse in ice cold water. This will cause the skins of the tomatoes to easily slip off, leaving the flesh intact. Remove cores and chop tomatoes. Put chopped tomatoes in slow cooker. Add all remaining ingredients. Cover with lid and cook on low for 7-9 hours. Remove slow cooker from heat source and let cool. When vegetables are cool, begin by pureeing 1 to 2 cups vegetables with broth, in blender. Return pureed mixture to slow cooker. Continue using the blender until all vegetables have been pureed. Stir to blend well. Pour into ice-cube freezer trays and freeze, then store frozen cubes in a freezer bag. Or this stock can be put in freezer containers or in pint/quart canning jars and processed for future use.

Harvest Stock

Prep. Time: about 25 minutes • Cost: about 13-cents per serving

4 turnips, peeled and chopped

3 cups shredded cabbage

10 medium to large ripe tomatoes

2 leeks, chopped

2 onions, quartered

1 head broccoli, chopped

1 green pepper, seeds removed, chopped

3 stalks celery, chopped

2 cloves garlic, peeled

2 teaspoons salt

½ teaspoon seasoned salt

1 teaspoon black pepper

1 teaspoon dried basil

1 teaspoon dried parsley

In large pan, bring about 2 quarts of water to a fast boil. Drop tomatoes in boiling water, 2 or 3 at a time and let cook for 30-45 seconds. Remove tomatoes and immerse in ice cold water. This will cause the skins of the tomatoes to easily slip off, leaving the flesh intact. Remove cores and chop tomatoes. Put chopped tomatoes in slow cooker. Combine all ingredients in slow cooker. Cover with lid and cook on low for 7-9 hours. Remove slow cooker from heat source and let cool. When vegetables are cool, begin by pureeing 1 to 2 cups vegetables with broth, in blender. Return pureed mixture to slow cooker. Continue using the blender until all vegetables have been pureed. Stir to blend well. Pour into ice-cube freezer trays and freeze, then store frozen cubes in a freezer bag. Or this stock can be put in freezer containers or in pint/quart canning jars and processed for future use.

About the Author:

Penny E. Stone relies on her slow cookers for providing home-cooked meals for her family of five. "With all I've got going on with my plate of daily responsibilities and activities, my slow cookers have become a lifesaver—especially since it's been a priority for me to keep my family connected and together during dinner-time." Penny is active in ABWA (American Business Women's Association); FYREHOUSE Ministries, a division of East Central Indiana Youth for Christ and her church as a Sunday School teacher. Her career in writing and promoting her books rounds out her full schedule. She and her husband reside in central Indiana with their three children, a dog, a cat, and several fish.

Index

LIFESTYLE SOLUTIONS

Crazy About Crockery!

101 Recipes for Entertaining at Less than .75¢ a serving

Penny E. Stone

Crazy About Crockery

101 Quick, Easy & Inexpensive Recipes for Entertaining at Less than .75 Cents a Serving

Penny E. Stone

Also by Penny E. Stone

CRAZY ABOUT CROCKERY: 101 Soup & Stew Recipes for Less than .75 cents a serving

CRAZY ABOUT CROCKERY: 101 Recipes for Entertaining at Less than .75 cents a serving

CRAZY ABOUT CROCKERY: 101 Easy & Inexpensive Recipes for Less than .75 cents a serving

365 Quick, Easy & Inexpensive Dinner Menus

CHAMPION PRESS, LTD.
FREDONIA, WISCONSIn

ISBN 1-891400-53-3 ~ LCCN 2002103113
Manufactured in Canada 10 9 8 7 6 5 4 3 2

Book Design by Kathy Campbell, Wildwood Studios

Introduction

I f you've been less than excited by the thought of entertaining... you're not alone! Most people are not natural-born-entertainers and shy away from "having company over," fearing all the preparation and work required. Minds are filled with visions of house-cleaning and slaving all day at a hot stove. Entertaining does not have to be that way. Your slow cooker is capable of making many recipes that can make entertaining a breeze. In this collection you'll find 101 of them! So relax... enjoy time and money-savings while creating scrumptious menus for your guests.

Please see page 94 for a complete recipe index.

SECTION I

Entrees for Dinner Guests

Each of the following recipes have been "tried and true" for me as I've prepared meals for church carry-in dinners, progressive dinners, and family potlucks. And each recipe can be made for less than .75-cents per serving. Actually, most of these recipes can be made for a lot less! So go ahead, pick up that phone, and invite some guests to join you for dinner!

Beef

WILD RICE AND BEEF

Prep. Time: 15 minutes • Serves 8+ • Cost: about 59-cents per serving

2 lbs. beef stew meat or leftover roast, torn in pieces
2 medium onions, finely chopped
1 teaspoon minced garlic
4½ cups boiling water
2¼ cups uncooked wild rice blend
2 cans cream of mushroom soup
1 large can (16 oz.) mushroom pieces or slices, plus liquid
1 teaspoon salt
1 teaspoon seasoned salt
2 teaspoons celery seed or flakes
2 teaspoons onion powder
2 teaspoons paprika
2 teaspoons coarse black pepper
1 bay leaf
2 cups Parmesan & Romano cheese topping

Combine boiling water with rice in your slow cooker. Let set for 20 minutes. Add all remaining ingredients. Stir to blend well. Cover with lid and cook on high for 7 hours.

MIDWEST BEEF CASSEROLE

Prep. Time: 20 minutes • Serves 6+ • Cost: about 69-cents per serving

1 lb. beef stew meat, cut in½ inch pieces
1 onion, chopped
2 cups water
4 beef bouillon cubes or 2 teaspoons beef seasoning mix
4 carrots, diced
1 can corn, drained
1 can red kidney beans, drained
3 cups cooked elbow macaroni or shells
2 cups cheddar cheese sauce or 2 cans Campbell's Cheese
  Soup®, undiluted

Chop beef in small pieces and put in slow cooker. Add chopped onion, water, beef bouillon and carrots. Cover and cook on high for 3-4 hours. Add corn and kidney beans; stir to mix well. Reduce heat to low and continue cooking for 3 more hours. Add drained cooked macaroni and cheese sauce (or soup). Stir to blend well. Cover with lid and continue cooking for about 30minutes to heat the macaroni and cheese. Stir well before serving. Season to taste.

TIMING IS EVERYTHING

Cheese should be served at room temperature. Keep cheese refrigerated until the day of the get-together. For soft cheeses, take them out of the refrigerator anywhere between 30 minutes to an hour before your guests are scheduled to arrive. For hard cheeses, pull them out of the refrigerator anywhere between two to three hours ahead of time. To keep cheeses from drying out or turning hard,
keep them covered with plastic wrap.

MENG POT ROAST

Prep. Time: 20 minutes Serving: 8 Cost: about 72-cents per serving

3-4 lb. beef roast, cut in chunks
1 teaspoon salt
2 teaspoons pepper
1 teaspoon paprika
1 teaspoon ground ginger
1 teaspoon dried thyme, crumbled
2 medium onions, chopped
1 medium carrot, grated
2 cup minced celery with leaves
1½ cups tomato juice
8 tablespoons soy sauce
2 teaspoons sugar
2 cups cold water with 3 tablespoons cornstarch dissolved in it
10-15 small red potatoes, scrubbed clean
3 - 4 medium carrots, cleaned and cut into bite-sized pieces
1 small can water chestnuts, drained

In a slow cooker combine salt, pepper, paprika, ginger, thyme, tomato juice, soy sauce, sugar and water with dissolved cornstarch. Stir to blend well. Add chunks of meat with chopped onions, grated carrot, and minced celery. Cover with lid and cook on high for 4 hours. Add red potatoes, chopped carrots, and drained water chestnuts. Cover with lid and continue cooking for an additional 3 - 4 hours. Serve when vegetables are tender and cooked through.

CREAMY BEEF 'N' MUSHROOMS CASSEROLE

Prep. Time: 15-20 minutes • Servings: 6-8 • Cost: about 68-cents per serving

2 lbs. round steak, cut in cubes
1 large onion, chopped
1 clove garlic, chopped
2 cups fresh mushrooms, sliced
2 cups celery, sliced
2 cups water
1 tablespoon butter or margarine
1 cup sour cream
1 teaspoon salt
¼ teaspoon black pepper
1 tablespoon Worcestershire sauce

In skillet, melt butter or margarine and saute onion, garlic, and celery until onion turns transparent. Transfer vegetables to slow cooker. Add beef , water, salt and Worcestershire sauce. Stir to blend well. Cover with lid and cook on low for 7-9 hours. Add mushrooms the last hour of cooking. Stir in sour cream and adjust seasonings when ready to serve. Serve over cooked rice or noodles.

HARVEST BEEF CASSEROLE

Prep. Time: 15 minutes Servings: 6-8 Cost: about 71-cents per serving

2 lbs. beef stew meat or round steak cut in pieces
2 medium onions, chopped
1 green pepper, chopped
2 stalks celery, chopped
2 teaspoons salt
2 teaspoons basil
2 teaspoons oregano
2 teaspoons sugar
2 teaspoons black pepper
2 teaspoons garlic powder
1 can (8 oz) red kidney beans, drained
1 can (8 oz) golden yellow hominy or sweet corn, drained
1 can (8 oz) green beans, drained
2 cans condensed tomato soup
1 soup can water
2 cups shredded cheddar cheese

Combine all ingredients, except the cheese, in the slow cooker. Stir to blend well. Cover with lid and cook on low for 8 hours. Pour contents of your slow cooker into serving bowl and top with shredded cheddar cheese. Serve immediately.

BBQ BEEF FOR SANDWICHES

Prep. Time: 20 minutes + Servings: 8+ Cost: about 58-cents per serving

3-4 lb. beef roast
2 cups water
2 onions; 1-sliced & 1-finely chopped
1 teaspoon salt
Prepared BBQ sauce

Place roast in slow cooker. Slice one onion and place rings over the top of the meat. Add 2 cups water and salt. Cover with lid and let cook on high for 7 hours. Remove roast from slow cooker and pour onions and cooking juices through a sieve. Save the clear beef broth for another recipe in refrigerator or freezer. Tear meat into shreds, discarding any gristle, fat, or bones. Return shredded meat toslow cooker. Add prepared BBQ sauce and stir to blend well. Cover with lid and continue cooking (to allow flavors to blend) on low for 1-2 hours. Serve on buns.

LASAGNA ROLLS

Prep. Time: about 30 minutes • Servings: 8+ • Cost: about 66-cents per serving

2 lbs. lean ground beef (or turkey)
2 cups (fresh) tomatoes, skins removed, diced, or 2 cups stewed
    tomatoes with juice
1 cup onions, chopped finely
1 can mushrooms, drained (small or large—your choice)
2 teaspoons oregano
2 teaspoons salt
½ teaspoon black pepper
2 cans (8 oz) tomato sauce
1 clove garlic, minced
2 teaspoons basil
2 bay leaves
2 teaspoons Italian seasoning

Brown ground beef in skillet with 1 teaspoon salt and onion. Drain off all grease. Spoon meat mixture into slow cooker. Add tomatoes, seasonings, and tomato sauce. Cover with lid and cook on high for 4 hours.

Cheese Filling

3 cups ricotta cheese
2 cups shredded or grated Romano cheese
2 cups shredded mozzarella cheese
2 tablespoons parsley flakes
½ teaspoon pepper
½ teaspoon salt
1 teaspoon garlic powder
2 eggs, beaten

In bowl combine all ingredients for cheese filling. Mix well.

1-2 pkgs. (16 oz) lasagna noodles

Prepare lasagna noodles according to package directions and rinse in cold water when almost tender. Do not cook lasagna noodles until tender. Drain noodles and pat dry with a paper towel. Spoon cheese mixture over the length of each lasagna noodle and roll up. Secure roll with a toothpick. Drop each filled lasagna roll in to the tomato sauce mixture. Turn heat down to low, cover with lid, and let rolls simmer in sauce for about an hour. Remove bay leaves before serving. Top with additional cheese if desired.

CROWD PLEASIN' BEEF CASSEROLE

Prep. Time: about 30 minutes • Serves: 36 • Cost: about 48-cents per serving

3 lbs. lean ground beef
2 lbs. lean skinless link sausages, diced
3 large onions, chopped
3 stalks celery, diced
1 green pepper, diced
3 cans tomato soup
1 bottle (12 oz.) chili sauce
2 teaspoons chili powder
2 teaspoons salt
½ teaspoon black pepper
2 cups water
¼ cup butter or margarine
2 cups American cheese, shredded or cubed
2 cups cheddar cheese, shredded or cubed
2 pkgs. medium noodles, cooked separately

In large skillet, cook ground beef with onions and green pepper. Drain off all grease when meat is cooked. Crumble beef and vegetables into slow cooker. Add all remaining ingredients except for the noodles. Cover with lid and cook on high for 7 hours. Serve over cooked noodles. Any leftovers may be frozen and reheated for another meal. Serves 36.

SPICED CORNED BEEF GLAZED IN CRANBERRY-WINE SAUCE

Prep. Time: about 10 minutes • Serves: 6+ • Cost: about 72-cents per serving

5-6 lbs. corned beef brisket
1 large onion, quartered
1 carrot, sliced
2 bay leaves
½ teaspoon whole black peppercorns, crushed
1 teaspoon whole allspice
1 teaspoon whole cloves
Water
1 can (8 oz.) whole cranberry sauce
1 cup red wine
1 teaspoon horseradish
2 teaspoons hot mustard
1 orange, grated peel and juice

Place beef brisket in slow cooker and cover with water. Add onion, carrot, bay leaves, pepper, allspice, and cloves. Cover with lid and cook on high for 8-10 hours. Remove from slow cooker and allow meat to cool. Slice meat into thin pieces and arrange on a platter. In saucepan, combine cranberry sauce, red wine, horseradish, hot mustard and orange juice and peel. Stir to blend well while heating over medium high heat. When sauce begins to boil, remove pan from heat and dip glaze over sliced beef. Serve immediately.

PENNY'S PEPPER 'N' RICE CASSEROLE

Prep. Time: about 20 minutes • Serves: 8+ • Cost: about 46-cents per serving

1½ - 2 lbs. lean ground beef
1 large onion, finely chopped
2 large green peppers, sliced into strips
6 cups stewed tomatoes with juice
1 cup water
6 cups uncooked instant rice
2 teaspoons salt
½ teaspoon pepper
2-3 cups shredded cheddar cheese

In skillet, brown ground beef with onion. Drain off all grease when beef is cooked. Crumble beef and onion into slow cooker. Puree tomatoes in blender, then pour into slow cooker.. Add green pepper, rice, salt and pepper. Stir to blend well. Cover with lid and cook on low for 6-8 hours. Serve. Sprinkle shredded cheddar cheese over each serving.

THREE-BEAN CASSEROLE

Prep. Time: about 20 minutes • Serves: 6+ • Cost: about 39-cents per serving

2 cans red kidney beans, drained
2 cans garbanzo beans, drained
2 cans black beans, drained
1½ to 2 lbs. ground beef
1 large onion, finely chopped
1 clove garlic, minced
2 cups brown sugar
2 teaspoons chili powder
2 tablespoons prepared mustard
2 cups ketchup
1 teaspoon ground cumin
2 teaspoons salt
½ teaspoon pepper

In skillet, brown ground beef with chopped onion. Drain off all grease. Crumble ground beef into slow cooker. Add beans and their canned liquids. Add remaining ingredients and stir to blend well. Cover with lid and cook on low for 6-7 hours.

BEEF ROAST WITH ONION-MUSHROOM GRAVY

Prep. Time: about 15 minutes • Serves: 6+ • Cost: about 61-cents per serving

3 to 4 lb beef roast, trimmed of excess fat
1 envelope Lipton dry onion soup mix
2 tablespoons A-1 Sauce™
2 cans cream of mushroom soup
1 soup can water
1 teaspoon salt
1 onion, chopped
2 cups fresh sliced mushrooms

Place roast in slow cooker. In a separate container, combine dry onion soup mix with A-1 Sauce™, cream of mushroom soup, water, salt, chopped onion and sliced mushrooms. Pour over meat. Cover with lid and cook on high for 7-9 hours.

CHILI STEAK

Prep. Time: about 10 minutes • Serves: 6+ • Cost: about 59-cents per serving

2 lbs. or more round steak
1 large onion, chopped
1 teaspoon salt
¼ teaspoon black pepper
2 cups prepared chili sauce OR 2 cups home-made chili sauce
2 cups water

Place a thin layer of onion on the bottom of slow cooker. Cut up meat into serving sized pieces. Sprinkle meat with salt and pepper. Place meat in slow cooker. Add chili sauce and water. Cover with lid and cook on low for 7 hours. Serve over baked potatoes, topped with cheddar cheese.

Party Time Meatballs

Prep. Time: about 30-45 minutes • Serves: 8+ • Cost: about 41-cents per serving

3-5 lbs. lean ground beef
2 tablespoons parsley flakes
1 teaspoon garlic powder
3 tablespoons minced onion
2 tablespoons Worcestershire sauce
2 teaspoon salt
½ teaspoon black pepper

Sauce Options:
CHILI
1 jar (10 oz.) grape jelly
1 bottle (12 oz.) chili sauce
        or
ITALIAN
1 can (8-10 oz.) pizza sauce
1 jar or can (about 15 oz.) spaghetti sauce
        or
MIDWEST
2 cans tomato soup
1 can cream of mushroom soup
1½ cups water
2 tablespoons steak sauce

In bowl, combine ground beef with meatball seasonings and mix well. Form into 2- inch balls. Cover a baking dish or rimmed cookie sheet with aluminum foil (this if for super easy cleanup!). Place meatballs on pan and place in oven. Broil for 3-5 minutes then turn meatballs over. Continue broiling for 3-5 minutes. When meatballs are browned, remove from oven. In the slow cooker, combine your choice of sauce ingredients of mix well. Add browned meatballs. Cover with lid and cook on low for up to 5 hours. (Serve after cooking on low for at least 2 hours.)

STEAK AND TOMATOES

Prep. Time: about 5 minutes • Serves: 6+ • Cost: about 41-cents per serving

2-3 lbs. round steak, trimmed of fat
2 cups stewed tomatoes with juice
1 onion, chopped
¼ cup diced green pepper
1 cup water
1 teaspoon salt
¼ teaspoon pepper

Place meat in slow cooker. Cover with chopped onions and green pepper. Cover with tomatoes. Add water, salt and pepper. Cover with lid and cook on high for 6-7 hours.

CHUCK ROAST WITH SOUR CREAM GRAVY

Prep. Time: about 15 minutes Serves: 6+ Cost: about 53-cents per serving

3-5 lb. chuck roast
2 cans cream of mushroom soup
1 onion, finely chopped
2 tablespoons cornstarch
1½ cups water
1½ cups sour cream or plain yogurt
2 teaspoons salt
¼ teaspoon pepper

Dissolve cornstarch in water. Combine soup, water, onion, 1½ teaspoons salt, and pepper in slow cooker. Stir to blend well. Add meat. Spoon soup mixture over meat. Sprinkle meat with remaining salt. Cover with lid and cook on high for 6-7 hours or on low for 8-9 hours. Remove meat from slow cooker and cut into serving pieces. Add sour cream to slow cooker mixture and stir to blend well. Serve gravy over each serving of meat.

GINGER BEEF WITH BROCCOLI

Prep. Time: about 10 minutes • Servings: 8+ • Cost: about 51-cents per serving

2-5 lbs. lean round steak, cut into serving portions
4-6 slices fresh ginger root
2 tablespoons soy sauce
1 teaspoon salt
12 green onions, chopped (including green tops)
2 bunches fresh broccoli, cut in spears
2 teaspoons cornstarch
1 cup cold water
2 teaspoons Kitchen Bouquet® (Browning & Seasoning Sauce)

Place pieces of meat in slow cooker. Add ginger root and green onions over meat. Drizzle soy sauce over meat. Dissolve cornstarch in cup of cold water and stir in Kitchen Bouquet. Pour over contents in slow cooker. Cover with lid and cook on high for 4 hours. Add broccoli to slow cooker. Sprinkle with salt. Cover and cook on low for another 3 hours.

PLUM-GOOD CUBED BEEF

Prep. Time: about 10 minutes • Serves: 6+ • Cost: about 56-cents per serving

1pc. of cubed beef per serving
1 cup babyfood plums
½ cup sugar
1 cup tomato sauce
3 tablespoons steak sauce
1 cup flour
1 teaspoon salt
½ teaspoon pepper

In bowl, combine flour with salt and pepper. Rinse off each piece of cubed beef with water and dredge through the flour mixture. In separate container, combine remaining ingredients. Layer meat and sauce in slow cooker. Cover with lid and cook on low for 6-7 hours.

One-Pot Chicken Meals

"SOUPER" CHICKEN AND RICE

Prep. Time: 15 minutes • Serves: 8+ • Cost: about 63-cents per serving

4 whole chicken breasts, split, skin removed
1 can cream of mushroom soup
1 can cream of celery soup
1 can cream of chicken soup
2 tablespoons butter
1 cup celery, sliced thin
1 onion, chopped finely
2 cups frozen peas
4½ cups uncooked instant rice
2 cups water
1½ teaspoons salt
½ teaspoon pepper

Combine soups, water, butter, celery, onion, salt, and pepper together in slow cooker. Immerse chicken breasts in soup mixture and cover slow cooker with lid. Cook on high for 5-6 hours. Remove chicken from slow cooker and add rice and peas to soup mixture. Stir. Cut chicken breasts in to bite-sized pieces and add back to slow cooker. Stir together. Cover with lid. Let mixture set for 10-15 minutes. Serve after rice fluffs up.

Seasoned Chicken and Rice

Prep. Time: 15 minutes • Serves: 8+ • Cost: about 65-cents per serving

4 whole chicken breasts, split, skin removed
1 can cream of mushroom soup
1 pkg. dry onion soup mix
1 can cream of celery soup
2 cups water
3 cups uncooked instant rice
1 cup celery, finely sliced
1 cup fresh mushrooms, sliced
2 sliced green bell peppers
1 teaspoon salt
1 tablespoon parsley flakes

In slow cooker, combine water and dry onion soup mix. Stir until dissolved. Add chicken breasts. Top with chopped celery. Cover with lid and cook on high for 6 hours. Remove chicken from slow cooker. Add in creamed soups, salt, parsley flakes, mushrooms, and green pepper. Cut chicken into strips. Add to slow cooker and stir to blend well. Cover with lid and let cook on high for another 1-2 hours. About 30 minutes before serving, add instant rice and stir to blend well. Cover with lid. Unplug slow cooker and set on table. Leave lid on slow cooker for at least 15 minutes before serving.

Chicken Tetrazzini

Prep. Time: about 20 minutes • Serves: 6+ • Cost: about 64-cents per serving

4 whole chicken breasts, split, skinless
2 cans cream of chicken soup
1 can cream of mushroom soup
1 cup milk
1 cup water
1 tablespoon dried minced onion
2 cups shredded cheddar cheese
1 pkg. (8 oz) spaghetti pasta or other shaped pasta
2 teaspoons parsley flakes
2 teaspoons basil
1 tablespoon Worcestershire Sauce
1 cup sour cream or plain yogurt
1 teaspoon salt
½ teaspoon coarse black pepper

Place chicken breasts in slow cooker. Cover with cream of chicken soup and 1 cup water. Cover with lid and cook on high for 6 hours. Remove chicken and cut into bite-sized pieces. Return chicken to slow cooker. Add all remaining ingredients except pasta and cheese. Cover slow cooker and reduce heat to low. Continue cooking for 1-3 hours. About 30 minutes prior to serving, stir in sour cream. In separate saucepan, prepare pasta according to package directions. Cook until tender, but firm. Rinse and drain. Serve slow cooker mixture over pasta. Top with shredded cheese.

CHICKEN GARDEN CASSEROLE

Prep. Time: about 20 minutes • Serves: 6+ • Cost: about 70-cents per serving

2-3 lbs. chicken, cut up, skin removed
2 tablespoons butter or margarine
1 cup finely chopped green pepper
1 cup diced celery
1 medium onion, finely chopped
1 can cream of mushroom soup
1 can cream of chicken soup
1 cup sliced mushrooms
2 cups chopped broccoli
2 carrots, diced
¼ cup slivered almonds
2 lb. processed American cheese
1 pkg. medium-wide egg noodles, cooked according to package
   directions

In small skillet, sauté green pepper, celery and onion in butter.
Cook until vegetables begin to turn tender. Pour vegetables and
butter into slow cooker. Add all remaining ingredients except for
almonds, cheese and noodles. Cover with lid and cook on high for
7 hours. Cut American cheese into cubes and add to slow
cooker. Stir to mix well. Cover with lid and let cook while you
prepare noodles according to package directions on stove top.
Serve casserole over a bed of cooked noodles. Top with the
slivered almonds as a garnish.

Neapolitan Chicken

Prep. Time: about 10 minutes • Serves: 6+ • Cost: about 47-cents per serving

1-2 whole chickens, cut into pieces
½ cup oil
1 tablespoon oregano
2 large sweet onions, sliced
2 cloves garlic, sliced
1 large can tomato puree
1 can water
1 teaspoon dried parsley flakes
2 teaspoons dried basil
1 teaspoon salt
½ teaspoon pepper

Arrange meat in slow cooker. Drizzle oil over all. Add remaining ingredients and cover with lid. Cook on low for 6-8 hours.

INEXPENSIVE DECORATING IDEAS

Make a professional-looking presentation with old paint cans, clay pots, empty buckets, etc. How? You ask. Easy! Cover your serving table with a tablecloth (don't use a plastic-vinyl cloth if you plan to set your slow cooker directly on it—instead use cloth). Next arrange those containers in the center by stacking some and making several different heights with flat surfaces. Then cover these unsightly containers with another tablecloth or piece of material, tucking it in under the bases of cans, buckets, or pots to keep it in place. Add serving trays to the protruding flat surfaces. Decorate with greenery and fresh flowers. Voila! No one will ever know what you really used on that table! One word of caution: keep your slow cooker on the base level of the table. Don't risk placing it on an elevated surface. There's a couple of reasons for this. 1) You increase the chances of someone getting burned by placing your slow cooker where people need to reach up and over to get to the contents. And 2) you want to protect your slow cooker from toppling over and breaking by suspending it on an elevated surface.

Seasoned Chicken Breasts

Prep. Time: about 15 minutes • Serves: 6+ • Cost: about 54-cents per serving

6+ boneless, skinless chicken breasts (enough for one per person)
1 pkg. dried beef
1 lb. bacon
2 cans cream of chicken soup
Salt and pepper to taste

Spray the insides of the slow cooker with non-stick vegetable spray. Overlap pieces of dried beef and cover the bottom and sides of the slow cooker. Wrap each piece of chicken with uncooked bacon. Secure bacon with tooth picks. Lay bacon wrapped chicken on dried beef in slow cooker. Cover all with undiluted cream of chicken soup. Cover with lid and cook on low for 7 hours. Unwrap chicken pieces and serve. Salt and pepper each piece of chicken according to your tastes.

HOOSIER CHICKEN CASSEROLE

Prep. Time: about 20 minutes • Serves: 6+ • Cost: about 73-cents per serving

1 whole chicken, skin removed, cut up
1 onion, chopped
2 stalks celery, sliced
4 cups water
2 teaspoons salt
½ teaspoon black pepper
½ stick butter
2 eggs, beaten
1 can cream of mushroom soup
1 can cream of chicken soup
1 can cream of celery soup
2 cups milk
1 teaspoon minced garlic
1 cup water chestnuts, drained and chopped
4 carrots, sliced
2 cups green beans (French cut looks nice)
½ cup toasted slivered almonds, optional
2 pkgs. Chicken-seasoned stuffing mix
2 cups shredded sharp cheddar cheese

Place cut up chicken in slow cooker. Add 4 cups water, 2 teaspoons salt, chopped onion, celery, and sliced carrots. Cover with lid and cook on high for 5 hours. Remove meat from slow cooker and let cool slightly. Add all remaining ingredients except stuffing mixes and cheese. Remove chicken from bone and tear into bite-sized pieces. Return chicken to slow cooker. Stir to blend well. Cover with lid, reduce heat to low, and continue cooking for 2-4 hours, Add stuffing mixes and mix well. Let set for 10 minutes. Add cheese, stir to blend well, then serve while hot.

GARLIC CHICKEN PICCATA

Prep. Time: about 15-20 minutes • Serves: 6+ • Cost: about 48-cents per serving

2 whole chickens, cut up, skin removed
1 teaspoon oregano
1 cup chicken broth
1 teaspoon salt
¼ teaspoon black pepper
2 cloves garlic, minced
1 cup apple juice
½ cup water
1 large onion, sliced
1 green pepper, sliced in rings
1 cup whole button mushrooms
2 cups shredded Cheddar cheese

Combine chicken broth and apple juice in slow cooker. Add garlic, oregano, salt and pepper. Stir well. Dip each piece of chicken in slow cooker and swish around, coating each piece with the liquid and herbs. After all pieces have been dipped, arrange chicken in slow cooker. Cover chicken with onion and green pepper rings. Cover with lid and cook on high for 5 hours. Add mushrooms and let cook, covered, for another hour. Smother each piece of chicken with shredded cheddar cheese when serving.

LEMON-HERB CHICKEN BREASTS

Prep. Time: about 15 minutes • Serves: 6+ • Cost: about 42-cents per serving

Chicken breasts, skinless, boneless (enough for 1 per person)
Juice from 2 fresh lemons plus enough water to equal 2 cups
Zest from 2 lemons (grated lemon rind, without the white)
½ teaspoon garlic powder
½ teaspoon salt
1/8 teaspoon cayenne (red) pepper
1 teaspoon celery flakes
1 teaspoon parsley flakes
¼ teaspoon seasoned salt
2 cups chicken broth

Pour chicken broth in slow cooker. Add seasoned salt, parsley & celery flakes, red pepper, salt and garlic powder. Stir to blend well. Dip each piece of chicken in seasoned broth, coating each piece with seasonings. Set aside until all pieces have been dipped. Add lemon juice to broth. Sprinkle lemon zest on each piece of chicken. Arrange chicken in slow cooker. Cover with lid and let cook on low for 6-8 hours.

HONEY-MUSTARD CHICKEN

Prep. Time: about 15 minutes • Serves: 6+ • Cost: about 48-cents per serving

2-4 lbs. chicken, cut up
1 cup water
1 cup honey
½ cup light brown sugar, firmly packed
3 tablespoons prepared Dijon mustard
2 tablespoons lemon juice
Salt

Remove skin from each piece of chicken. Rub Dijon mustard over each piece. Arrange chicken in slow cooker. Sprinkle brown sugar over each piece. Drizzle with honey. Combine lemon juice with water and pour in slow cooker at the side, being careful not to rinse off the brown sugar and honey on the chicken pieces. Generously sprinkle salt over chicken. Cover with lid and cook on low for 6-8 hours.

GREAT GARNISHES

Wash and spin dry or pat dry greens the day of the party. Store them in a brown paper bag in the refrigerator until you're ready to set out the food. At that time, and not before, break off twigs and pieces of greenery for garnishes. Good greens to use include fresh moss-curled parsley, French tarragon, Rosemary, and different varieties of lettuce.

Edible flowers make great garnishes! Combine the flower bloom with the greenery of herbs and you've got a totally edible garnish that is pleasing to the sense of sight, smell, and taste! Marigolds, violets, dandelions, squash blooms, and nasturtiums are just some of the edible flowers you can use. When sliced hard-boiled eggs for a garnish, wet the knife before slicing. The wet blade helps prevent the yolk from crumbing when cut.

Radish rosettes, carrot and celery sticks, green onion wands, and other vegetables cut to design will stay fresh and crisp if stored immersed in water in the refrigerator. Be sure to drain and pat dry when you're ready to use them.

GREEK CHICKEN

Prep. Time: about 15 minutes • Serves: 6+ • Cost: about 47-cents per serving

2-4 lbs. chicken, cut up
½ teaspoon garlic powder
½ teaspoon oregano
¼ cup lemon juice
½ cup Olive Oil
1 onion, finely chopped
1 teaspoon seasoned salt
¼ teaspoon salt
½ teaspoon coarse black pepper

Cut up chicken and remove skin. Arrange in slow cooker. In separate container, combine Olive Oil with all remaining ingredients. Shake or stir well then pour over chicken pieces. Cover with lid and cook on low for 6-8 hours.

SLOW COOKER CHICKEN KIEV

Prep. Time: about 20 minutes • Serves: 6+ • Cost: about 47-cents per serving

3-4 lbs. chicken, cut up
¼-½ stick butter
3 tablespoons grated Parmesan cheese
1 teaspoon sweet basil
½ teaspoon oregano
½ teaspoon garlic powder
1 teaspoon seasoned salt
1 cup apple juice
1 bunch green onions, chopped
2 tablespoons fresh chopped parsley

In saucepan, melt butter and add Parmesan cheese, basil, oregano, garlic powder, and salt. Remove skin from each piece of chicken, then dip each piece in butter. Arrange coated chicken in slow cooker. Add apple juice, onion, and fresh parsley to slow cooker. Cover with lid and cook on low for 6 - 8 hours.

BACON & MUSHROOM CHICKEN

Prep. Time: about 20 minutes • Serves: 6+ • Cost: about 52-cents per serving

½ lb. bacon
2-4 lbs. chicken, cut up
1 cup flour
½ teaspoon salt
1 teaspoon seasoned salt
½ teaspoon black pepper
2 large onions, chopped
1 teaspoon garlic powder
2 cups fresh mushroom slices
2 cans stewed tomatoes
1 teaspoon parsley flakes

In skillet, fry bacon until crisp; set aside. In separate container, combine flour with seasoned salt, regular salt and pepper. Remove skin from each piece of chicken and rinse in warm water. Dredge each piece in flour mixture. Arrange coated chicken in hot bacon grease in skillet. Cook over medium heat for 5-7 minutes, browning on both sides. Remove chicken from skillet and arrange in slow cooker. Crumble crisp bacon over browned chicken pieces. Cover chicken with mushroom slices; next add chopped onion. Pour tomatoes in blender and whiz on high to puree and then pour over contents of slow cooker. Cover with lid and cook on high for 6 hours.

ITALIAN CHICKEN

Prep. Time: about 10-15 minutes • Serves: 6+ • Cost: about 54-cents per serving

3-4 lbs. chicken, cut up
½ - 1 stick butter or margarine OR 1 can (15 oz.) tomato sauce
1 teaspoon garlic powder
1 teaspoon oregano
1 teaspoon Italian seasoning
2 teaspoons dried parsley
2 teaspoons basil
1 teaspoon salt
½ teaspoon pepper
shredded Cheddar Cheese

Remove skin from each piece of chicken. In bowl, combine melted butter or margarine OR tomato sauce with remaining ingredients. Dip each piece of chicken in seasonings coating all sides; arrange pieces in slow cooker. Pour any remaining seasonings over chicken and cover with lid. Cook on high for 6 - 7 hours. Sprinkle cheddar cheese over each piece when served.

Glazed Chicken

Prep. Time: about 20 minutes • Serves: 6+ • Cost: about 53-cents per serving

3-4 lbs. chicken, cut up
1 jar (12 oz.) apricot preserves
2 tablespoons red wine vinegar
1 teaspoon salt
1/8 teaspoon pepper
½ cup orange juice
½ cup water
2 tablespoons light brown sugar

Remove skin from chicken and split each breast in half. Rinse in warm water and arrange in slow cooker. In separate container, combine all remaining ingredients; stir to blend well. Pour over each piece of chicken, being sure to coat each piece. Cover with lid and cook on high for 6 - 7 hours.

Chicken Tango

Prep. Time: about 15 minutes • Serves: 6+ • Cost: about 57- cents per serving

1 whole chicken, cut up, skin removed
2 extra chicken legs, skin removed
1 extra chicken breast, skin removed, cut in half
1 bottle of Russian Fat Free salad dressing
1 small jar apricot preserves
1 teaspoon salt
¼ teaspoon pepper
1 cup water, boiling

Place chicken in slow cooker. Pour the Russian salad dressing over each piece. Combine boiling water with the apricot preserves. Add the salt and pepper and mix well, then pour the thinned preserves over the chicken. Cover with lid and cook on low for 7-9 hours.

Sicilian Chicken

Prep. Time: about 10 minutes • Serves: 6+ • Cost: about 47-cents per serving

6-9 pieces of chicken, skin removed
½ - 1 stick butter or margarine
1 cup flour
½ teaspoon black pepper
1 tablespoon paprika
1½ teaspoons salt
2 cloves garlic, minced
1 cup water
2 cup snipped fresh parsley

Coat each piece of chicken with melted butter or margarine. In small bowl, combine flour, pepper, paprika, salt and garlic. Dredge each piece of meat through flour mixture. Pour remaining butter or margarine in skillet and brown chicken on all sides until lightly browned. Arrange chicken in slow cooker. Add 1 cup water. Cover with lid and cook on high for 6 hours. Remove meat from slow cooker and arrange on serving platter. Serve with cooked ziti covered in tomato or spaghetti sauce.

CALL AHEAD AND DON'T TAKE CHANCES

There's no reason to go to all the work of planning a dinner party only to discover the local grocery produce or meat department is out of the one ingredient you'd planned to center your meal around. So plan ahead and call ahead. Speak directly to either the produce manager or meat department manager and request the store have in stock the item(s) you're planning to serve. This not only will ensure you'll find what you need, but it also helps out the store managers in knowing for sure what they need to order to meet consumer demand.

CHILI BING CHICKEN

Prep. Time: about 15 minutes • Serves: 10+ • Cost: about 59-cents per serving

2 whole chickens, cut up, skin removed
2 teaspoons salt
½ teaspoon black pepper
1 teaspoon garlic powder
½ - 1 stick butter or margarine, melted
2 medium onions, chopped
1½ cups prepared chili sauce
1 cup sherry or wine
2 cups ripe Bing cherries, pitted and chopped
1 teaspoon Worcestershire sauce
¾ cup flour
2 cup yellow corn meal
1 teaspoon dried parsley flakes
1 teaspoon dried basil

Wash chicken and remove skin. In shallow dish, combine flour, corn meal, parsley, basil, salt, pepper and garlic powder. Lightly coat each piece of chicken in floured mixture. Melt butter or margarine in skillet and lightly brown all sides of each piece of chicken. Arrange browned chicken in slow cooker. Add onions and cherries over chicken. Add Worcestershire sauce to remaining butter or margarine. Stir to blend well. Drizzle seasoned butter over chicken pieces. Add chili sauce to slow cooker. Cover with lid and cook on high for 6-8 hours.

CHICKEN CURRY

Prep. Time: about 20 minutes • Serves: 6+ • Cost: about 57-cents per serving

6-9 pieces of chicken, skin removed
3 cups hot water
1 tablespoon salt
1 stalk celery, chopped
1 bay leaf
1 onion, quartered
2 tart apples, peeled, pared and diced
½ stick butter or margarine
1 teaspoon salt
3 teaspoons curry powder
½ teaspoon black pepper
½ cup flour
2 cups heavy cream

Arrange chicken in slow cooker. Add water, 1 tablespoon salt, celery, onion and bay leaf. Cover with lid and cook on high for 5 hours. Remove chicken from slow cooker and set aside to cool. Remove cooked onion and celery and puree in blender with a little bit of salted water. Discard remaining water and bay leaf from slow cooker. Melt butter or margarine in bottom of hot slow cooker. Stir in flour, 1 teaspoon salt, 3 teaspoons curry powder and ½ teaspoon black pepper. Immediately stir in cream. Reduce heat to low and let this seasoned mixture cook, uncovered, while you pick the chicken off the bones. Tear meat into bite-sized pieces and add to slow cooker mixture. Add chopped apples last. Cover with lid, reduce heat to low, and continue cooking for 2 hours. Serve over cooked rice.

BAKED CHICKEN WITH MUSHROOM GRAVY

Prep. Time: about 15 minutes • Serves: 10+ • Cost: about 47-cents per serving

2 whole chickens, cut up, washed
butter or margarine
2 teaspoons ground thyme
2 teaspoons crushed tarragon leaves
5 cups chicken broth
½ cup flour
2 small cans (4 oz) mushrooms, reserve liquid
1 teaspoon salt
½ teaspoon pepper

Rub each piece of chicken with butter. Sprinkle thyme, tarragon, salt and pepper over each piece. Place meat in slow cooker. Pour chicken broth over meat and cover with lid. Cook on high for 6 hours. In a large skillet, melt ½ cup butter over medium high heat. Stir in flour to make a paste and then add 3-4 cups chicken broth from slow cooker. Continue stirring and cooking over medium-high heat until mixture thickens. Add mushrooms with their liquid and cook until heated through. To serve, place chicken on a platter and pour mushroom gravy over chicken before serving. Gravy may be used over mashed potatoes, too.

Pork

SAHALMAZETTI

Prep. Time: about 15 minutes • Serves: 8+ • Cost: about 68-cents per serving

3-4 lbs. pork roast, cooked and shredded
2 cups chopped celery
2 medium onions, chopped
1 medium green pepper, sliced into rings
1 lb. processed American cheese, sliced thin
2 cans tomato soup
2 soup cans water
2 pkgs. wide egg noodles, cooked

In large bowl, combine meat with celery, onion, tomato soup and water; mix well. Form patties and place into slow cooker. Arrange green pepper slices over meat. Cover with lid and cook on high for 6 hours. Prepare egg noodles according to package directions; rinse in cold water when tender. In large casserole dish, arrange cooked noodles on bottom. Cover noodles with thin slices of American cheese. Pour contents from slow cooker over cheese and serve immediately.

MEXICAN BEAN CASSEROLE

Prep. Time: about 20 minutes • Serves: 6 • Cost: about 67-cents per serving

2-3 lbs. boneless pork, cut into cubes

2 lbs. black beans, cooked

2 onions, chopped

1 clove garlic, minced

2 cans (16 oz.) stewed tomatoes

2 teaspoons chili powder

1 teaspoon ground coriander

½ teaspoon ground cumin

2 teaspoons salt

½ - 1 teaspoon red pepper

2 tablespoons fresh cilantro

Prepare beans according to package directions. Put cooked beans in slow cooker. Add all remaining ingredients and stir to blend well. Cover with lid and cook on low for 9 hours.

MAKE DINNER A POTLUCK!

In today's society it seems we're busier now than ever before. So who has the time to plan and prepare a full fledged dinner party any more? Save yourself some stress and all the work by asking each of your guests to bring a covered dish for the meal. With everyone chipping in with at least one food item, this will save you not only in terms of money, but also in the amount of time it would take you otherwise to do all the cooking and clean-up.

When you invite your guests, ask them to bring along a couple empty margarine tubs with lids or whipped topping containers with lids. Then following the party, you can divide the leftovers and send a little bit of something home with each guest! Or visit your local oriental take-out restaurant and ask for several of their small empty cardboard containers. Fill these with leftovers and send them home with your guests.

SLOW COOKER CHOP SUEY

Prep. Time: about 15 minutes • Serves: 6+ • Cost: about 58-cents per serving

2-4 lbs. pork shoulder
1 cup water
4 tablespoons soy sauce
2 cans Chinese vegetables, drained
1 can bean sprouts, drained
1 can water chestnuts, chopped and drained
2 stalks celery, diced
2 medium onions, chopped
2 pkts. brown gravy mix
3 cups water

Place meat in slow cooker. Add 1 cup water and 2 tablespoons soy sauce, pouring over meat. Cover with lid and cook on high for 5 hours. Remove meat and set aside to cool. Drain off all meat drippings. Combine gravy mixes and 2 cups water and pour into slow cooker. Add drained vegetables, remaining 2 tablespoons soy sauce, and stir. Tear cooked meat into bite-sized portions and return meat to slow cooker. Cover with lid, reduce heat to low, and continue cooking for 2 more hours. Serve hot over cooked rice or Chow Mein noodles.

Garden Chop Suey

Prep. Time: 15-20 minutes • Servings: 8+ • Cost: about 72-cents per serving

2-4 lbs. fresh pork, cut into cubes
½ cup soy sauce
2 tablespoons cornstarch
1 pint (2 cups) carrot sticks or baby carrots
1 pint (2 cups) diced celery
1 pint (2 cups) chopped onion
1 pint (2 cups) finely chopped cabbage
2 cups fresh spinach, chopped
2 cup bean sprouts, drained
2 cups frozen peas or sugar snap peas
1 cup water chestnuts, chopped
4 cups water

Pour water in slow cooker. Add soy sauce and cornstarch, stir until cornstarch is dissolved. Add fresh vegetables and cubed pork. Stir to blend well. Cover with lid and cook on low for 7-9 hours.

ORGANIZATION IS THE KEY

Here's a tip from professional caterers——make lists and more lists! Make a list of each recipe you plan to serve, then make a second list of everything you'll need to make those recipes. Then create a shopping list. Make a list of everything you'll need for serving containers, place settings, serving spoons, etc. Make a list of the guests you plan to invite and keep track of who is coming and who can't. Make a list of all the chores that need done around the house in preparation for having guests in for a visit. Make a list of items you can delegate to others to do.

By organizing yourself with lists, you won't be caught off guard by something important not being done or forgotten. Be sure to give yourself plenty of time to accomplish everything that gets put on your "to do" lists!

SPICY PEPPERED PORK CASSEROLE

Prep. Time: 12-15 minutes • Servings: 8+ • Cost: about 73-cents per serving

2½ - 4 lbs. pork shoulder roast, trimmed of fat
2 cups water
2 teaspoons salt
2 cans (4 oz) diced green chili peppers
2 tablespoons hot salsa
2 jalapeno peppers, seeded, finely chopped
2½ teaspoon red pepper
1 teaspoon ground cumin
1 teaspoon chili powder
1 can black beans, rinsed and drained
1 can pinto beans, rinsed and drained
1 can (14.5 oz.) diced tomatoes
1 cup water
1 teaspoon salt
2 cups brown rice
2 cups shredded cheddar cheese
Sour cream, optional

Place meat in slow cooker and add 2 cups water and 2 teaspoons salt. Cover with lid and cook on high for 6 hours. Remove
meat from slow cooker and set aside to cool. Empty all contents
from slow cooker. Combine green chili peppers, salsa, chopped
jalapeno peppers, red pepper, cumin, chili powder, black and
pinto beans, diced tomatoes, 1 cup water, 1 teaspoon salt, and
brown rice in slow cooker. Tear pork into shreds and return meat
to slow cooker. Stir to blend well. Cover with lid and continue
cooking on high for 4 hours. Serve with sour cream if desired.

ITALIANO SAUSAGE CASSEROLE

Prep. Time: about 20 minutes • Serves: 6+ • Cost: about 63-cents per serving

1 lb. smoked sausage
1 lb. ground sausage, cooked, drained, and crumbled
2 large onions, finely chopped
1 can stewed tomatoes
2 small cans tomato paste
2 teaspoons dried basil
2 teaspoons dried oregano
2 teaspoons dried parsley
2 teaspoons salt
1 teaspoon sugar
½ cups Parmesan cheese
1 cup shredded sharp cheddar cheese
1 cup shredded mozzarella cheese
1-2 pkgs. medium-to-wide curly noodles

Cut smoked sausage into bite-sized pieces. Cook ground sausage and crumble into slow cooker. Add smoked sausage, chopped onions, stewed tomatoes, and seasonings. Stir to blend well. Cover with lid and cook on low for 4-6 hours. Prepare noodles according to package directions. Add noodles and cheeses and stir to blend well. Serve immediately.

HAM & POTATOES

Prep. Time: 15-20 minutes • Servings: 8+ • Cost: about 71-cents per serving

10 medium potatoes, peeled and sliced
1 teaspoon salt
½ teaspoon pepper
1 onion, chopped
2 lbs. baked ham, cut in thin strips or diced in small squares
1 pkg. instant dry onion soup mix
1 can cream of mushroom soup
1 soup can water
2 cups shredded cheddar cheese
1 cup American processed cheese spread

Combine all ingredients in slow cooker and mix well. Cover with lid and cook on low for 6 hours or until potatoes are tender.

BAKED HAM FOR COMPANY

Prep. Time: about 10 minutes • Serves: 6+ • Cost: about 42-cents per serving

1 ham, sliced
2 cups regular Coca-cola
1 can pineapple rings
1 cup ketchup

Slice ham so slices will fit in slow cooker. Arrange pineapple rings over meat. Combine Coca-Cola with remaining pineapple juice and ketchup. Pour over ham. Cover with lid and cook on low for 8-10 hours.

"BAKED" GLAZED HAM

Prep. Time: about 10 minutes • Serves: 6+ • Cost: about 51-cents per serving

Ham
Glaze:
1 cup brown sugar
1 tablespoon dry mustard
½ cup vinegar
½ cup water
1 can pineapple rings, juice reserved

Place ham in slow cooker. Pour pineapple juice over ham. In a small saucepan, combine brown sugar, dry mustard, vinegar and water. Bring to a boil over medium heat. Pour over ham. Arrange pineapple slices on ham. Securing, if necessary, with toothpicks. Cover with lid and cook on low for 8-10 hours.

CURRIED PORK SHOULDER

Prep. Time: about 15 minutes • Serves: 8+ • Cost: about 41-cents per serving

3-4 lbs. lean pork shoulder, cut into 1½ inch squares
2 tablespoons butter
3 cups chicken bouillon
1 large onion, sliced
1 cup sliced celery
1 teaspoon curry powder
2 teaspoons salt
½ teaspoon pepper

Combine butter and remaining ingredients except pork in slow cooker. Stir to blend well. Add pieces of pork. Cover with lid and cook on low for 7-9 hours. Serve over cooked noodles or rice.

BBQ PORK SHOULDER

Prep. Time: about 15 minutes • Serves: 8+ • Cost: about 59-cents per serving

1 (3-4 lbs.) pork shoulder roast
½ cup cider vinegar
1 small onion, finely chopped
1 teaspoon Worcestershire sauce
1 teaspoon hot pepper sauce, optional
1 teaspoon liquid smoke
¼ cup brown sugar
1 teaspoon salt
1 teaspoon paprika
¼ teaspoon pepper
½ cup ketchup

In a large bowl combine vinegar, onion, Worcestershire sauce and hot sauce. Stir to blend well. Add pork roast and turn to coat the meat in the sauce. Cover with plastic wrap and let meat marinate in refrigerator over night. The next morning, remove meat from marinade and set aside. Pour marinade into slow cooker and add Liquid Smoke. Stir to blend well then set meat in slow cooker.

In small bowl, combine the brown sugar, salt, paprika and pepper. Pour this mixture over the top of the pork roast and pat it into the meat. Cover with lid and cook on the low setting for 7 to 9 hours. When pork is very tender, remove meat and transfer meat to serving platter. Drain off liquid from slow cooker and set it in the refrigerator for an hour to separate. Strain off the fat and discard. Add ketchup to remaining liquid, taste and adjust seasonings according to taste. Use two forks to shred pork and then add the sauce. Stir to blend well. Serve on buns.

BBQ PORK

Prep. Time: about 15 minutes • Serves: 8+
• Cost: about 59-cents per serving

3 to 4 lbs. lean pork
Sauce:
1 teaspoon salt
¼ teaspoon cayenne pepper
1 teaspoon horseradish
½ teaspoon paprika
½ teaspoon chili powder
½ teaspoon dry mustard
½ cup brown sugar, firmly packed
1 teaspoon Worcestershire Sauce
2 tablespoons vinegar
1 cup water
½ cups ketchup
1 onion, diced

Set pork in slow cooker. In a separate container, combine all
ingredients for the sauce and stir to blend well. Pour sauce over
pork. Cover with lid and cook on high for 7 hours.

SEND GUESTS HOME WITH GOODIES

A nice touch for any get-together is to send your guests home with a
little something. This can be a few homemade cookies wrapped in tulle
and tied with a ribbon, some caramel corn in a brown lunch bag
decorated with buttons and a raffia bow, or homemade candy (like
fudge or divinity) in a Chinese take-out container
that has been decorated.

Sweet and Sour Pork

Prep. Time: about 20 minutes • Serves: 6+ • Cost: about 73-cents per serving

2-3 lbs. lean pork shoulder, cut into pieces
2 tablespoons oil
¼ cup water
½ cup brown sugar
2 tablespoons cornstarch
1 teaspoon salt
¼ cup vinegar
1 tablespoon soy sauce
1 can pineapple chunks, reserve juice
1 green pepper, cut julienne style
2 tomatoes, cut into eighths
1 peeled orange in chunks

Brown meat in hot oil and drain on paper towel. Combine water with brown sugar, cornstarch, salt, vinegar, and soy sauce with liquid from canned pineapple. Stir to blend well. Add browned meat and stir to coat meat in sauce. Cover with lid and cook on low for 6-7 hours. Add remaining ingredients and cook for an additional hour. Serve over cooked rice.

Mexican Pork

Prep. Time: about 20 minutes • Serves: 6+ • Cost: about 57-cents per serving

3-5 lbs. pork, (boneless pork chops, pork loin, tenderloin), cut into
bite-sized pieces
2 large onions, chopped
4 cloves garlic, chopped
1 can (16 oz.) tomatoes with liquid
2-3 jalapeno peppers, seeded and finely chopped
3 bay leaves
2 tablespoons chili powder
1 teaspoon ground cumin
1 teaspoon oregano
¼ teaspoon red pepper

Trim all visible fat from pork and place meat in slow cooker. Add
canned tomatoes with their liquid, onions, the garlic, jalapeno
peppers, bay leaves, chili powder, cumin, oregano and red
pepper. Cover with lid and cook on high for 6 hours. Discard bay
leaves. Shred pork by using two forks and pulling meat from
opposite directions. Stir shredded meat with seasonings; serve
with tortillas and your choice of toppings.

PORKY GOULASH

Prep. Time: 18-20 minutes • Servings: 6-8 • Cost: about 74-cents per serving

2-3 lbs. lean pork, trimmed of all fat, cut into bite-size pieces
1 smoked ham hock
½ green pepper, chopped
2 tablespoons minced onions
1 teaspoon oregano
2 teaspoons salt
4 medium or 3 large fresh ripe tomatoes, diced
8-10 new red potatoes, scrubbed clean (leave skins on)
2 lbs. fresh green beans, washed and snapped
1 can (15 oz.) beef broth
½ teaspoon paprika
1 clove garlic, minced

Place ham hock in center of slow cooker. Add green beans around and over ham hock. Add red potatoes and pork. In bowl, combine green pepper, minced onion, oregano, salt, paprika and minced garlic. Stir to blend well and sprinkle mixture over contents in slow cooker. Add beef broth. Cover with lid and cook on high for 6-8 hours. Remove ham hock and discard. Add diced tomatoes and stir to blend meat with vegetables. Serve immediately.

PIZZA SUPREME CASSEROLE

Prep. Time: about 20 minutes • Serves: 10+ • Cost: about 71-cents per serving

2 lbs. ground bulk sausage, cooked, drained, and crumbled
1 lb. ground pork, cooked, drained, and crumbled
2 large sweet onions, chopped
2 cups sliced mushrooms
1 diced green pepper
2 pkgs. dried egg noodles, medium to wide width
1 can or jar prepared spaghetti sauce
1 can or jar prepared pizza sauce
1 teaspoon salt
2 teaspoons Italian seasonings
1 teaspoon oregano
2 cups shredded mozzarella cheese
1 cup shredded cheddar cheese

Cook meats and drain. Add all ingredients to slow cooker except cheeses and noodles. Stir to mix well. Cover with lid and cook on low for 4-6 hours. Prepare noodles according to package directions. Combine slow cooker ingredients with cooked noodles when ready to serve. Top each serving generously with shredded cheeses.

SHOP YOURSELF

Unless you can make your shopping list so specific there's no question regarding substitutions, do the shopping yourself. By doing your own shopping you can make last minute substitutions based on something being on sale or quality factors. For example, if you plan to serve a tossed salad but find the tomatoes are all too soft and mushy and the lettuce looks a bit wilted, you may decide to serve a coleslaw or carrot-raisin salad instead.

BLOCK PARTY BEANS

Prep. Time: about 15 minutes • Serves: 8+ • Cost: about 49-cents per serving

2 lbs. ham, diced
1 smoked ham hock
1 large onion, finely chopped
1 stalk celery, finely chopped
1 can tomato soup
1 can tomato paste
½ cup ketchup
2 cans green beans, drained
2 cans waxed beans, drained
2 cans chili beans (undrained)
1 can pork 'n' beans
1 can red kidney beans
1 can great northern beans
1 cup brown sugar
2 tablespoons prepared mustard

Combine all ingredients in slow cooker. Cover with lid and cook on low for 6 hours. Remove ham hock before serving.

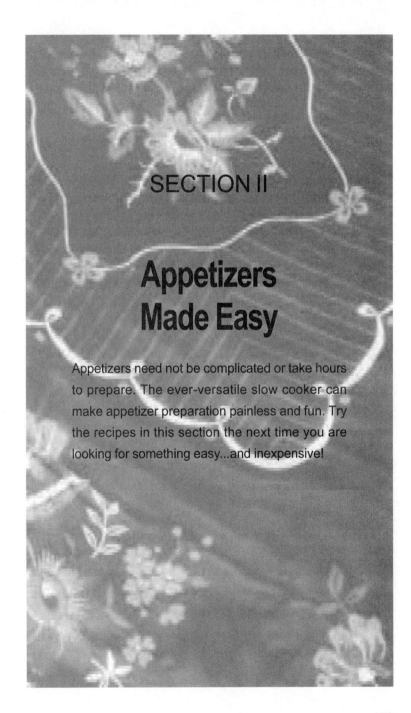

SECTION II

Appetizers Made Easy

Appetizers need not be complicated or take hours to prepare. The ever-versatile slow cooker can make appetizer preparation painless and fun. Try the recipes in this section the next time you are looking for something easy...and inexpensive!

CHILI BEAN DIP

Prep. Time: about 15-20 minutes • Serves: 6+ • Cost: about 39-cents per serving

2 cans (16 oz) fat free refried beans
1 lb. lean ground beef
1 medium onion, finely chopped
2 cans chopped chilies
2 cups chili sauce
2 cups shredded Monterey Jack cheese
2 cups shredded Sharp Colby cheese
1 pint sour cream
1 can sliced ripe (black) olives, drained

Brown meat with onion in a skillet. Drain off all grease. In slow cooker, combine refried beans with cooked meat and onion, chopped chilies, and chili sauce. Stir until well blended. Add cheeses and stir well. Cover with lid and let simmer on low for 4 hours. When ready to serve, mix in sour cream and black olives. Keep dip warm while serving. Use corn chips, taco chips, or other chips to serve.

Hot Cheese & Tomato Dip

Prep. Time: about 15 minutes • Serves: 6+ • Cost: about 39-cents per serving

1 lb. American cheese, cubed
1-2 lbs. bulk sausage, browned and drained
2 cups stewed tomatoes with juice
1 can hot chilies

Cook sausage in a skillet over medium heat until done. Drain off all grease. Combine cooked sausage and cubes of American cheese in slow cooker. Pour tomatoes in blender and puree a few seconds. Pour into slow cooker. Add chopped chilies to slow cooker. Stir well. Cover with lid and let simmer on low for 4-6 hours. Keep dip warm while serving.

Chili Cheese Tortilla Dip

Prep. Time: about 20 minutes • Serves: 10+ • Cost: about 29-cents per serving

1 can Hormel®Chili with no beans
3 lbs. American cheese, cut into cubes
1 lb. ground beef or turkey
1 large sweet onion, finely chopped
Salt and pepper according to taste

In skillet, sprinkle raw meat with salt and pepper. Cook meat with finely chopped onion until done. Drain off all grease. Crumble meat and onion into slow cooker. Add remaining ingredients to slow cooker. Cover with lid and cook on low for 4 hours or longer. Stir before serving. Dip tortilla chips into dip and enjoy!

Hot Bean Dip

Prep. Time: about 15 minutes • Serves: 6+ • Cost: about 41-cents per serving

1 (1 lb.) can pork 'n' beans
½ cup shredded sharp processed cheese
½ teaspoon garlic salt
dash cayenne pepper
1 teaspoon wine vinegar
¼ teaspoon liquid smoke
8 slices crisp bacon, crumbled

Pour beans into slow cooker and mash with a potato masher. Add all remaining ingredients except the bacon. Stir to blend well. Top mixture with crumbled bacon. Cover and cook on low for 4-6 hours. Keep dip warm while serving.

Hot and Spicy Chili Dip

Prep. Time: less than 5 minutes • Serves: 6+ • Cost: about 37-cents per serving

2 cans Hormel Chili® with no beans
3 lbs. American Cheese, cut into cubes
1 large jar Cheese Whiz®
1 small can (4 oz.) tomato sauce
½ pkg. Chili Seasoning Mix

Combine all ingredients in slow cooker. Cover with lid and cook on low for 4-6 hours. Stir before serving. If dip is too spicy, it may be "toned down" by adding 1-2 cups sour cream or plain yogurt. Or you may omit the chili seasoning mix and reduce the canned chili to one can. Stir to mix well. Keep dip warm while serving.

Spicy Cheese Dip

Prep. Time: less than 5 minutes • Serves: 6+ • Cost: about 34-cents per serving

2 lbs. American cheese, cut in cubes
1 small jar Cheese Whiz®
2 jars salsa (your choice of hot, medium, mild and chunky or
    regular)
1 tablespoon taco seasoning Mix

Combine all ingredients in slow cooker. Cover with lid and turn
control setting to high. Stir after every hour until ready to serve.
Once dip is well blended, turn heat control to low to keep warm
during party.

Nacho Cheese Dip

Prep. Time: about 15 minutes • Serves: 8+ • Cost: about 39-cents per serving

2 lbs. lean ground beef
2 cans (6 oz.) tomato paste
2 cans cream of mushroom soup
2 jars (16 oz.) salsa (your choice as to temperature)
2 lbs. Mexican Velveeta® cheese, cubed

In skillet, brown ground beef over medium-high heat. Drain off all
grease and crumble meat into slow cooker. Add remaining
ingredients. Cover with lid and cook on low for 4-6 hours. Keep
warm while serving.

Taco Nacho Cheese Dip

Prep. Time: about 15-20 minutes • Serves: 8+ • Cost: about 49-cents per serving

2 lbs. lean ground beef
1 large container (16 oz.) sour cream
1 lb. Mexican Velveeta® cheese, cubed
1 lb. American cheese, cubed
4 ripe tomatoes, chopped
1 pkt. taco seasoning mix

In skillet, brown ground been over medium-high heat. Drain off all grease and crumble meat into slow cooker. Add remaining ingredients, except for sour cream. Cover with lid and cook on low for 4-6 hours. Add sour cream and stir to blend well. Keep warm while serving.

Cheese Fondue

1 lb. Swiss cheese, in small pieces or cubed
1 lb. American cheese, cubed
4 tablespoons butter
1 teaspoon salt
2 cups milk
4 tablespoons flour
¼ teaspoon garlic powder
Cubed French bread for dipping

In pan or skillet on stovetop, melt butter and stir in flour to form a paste. Gradually add milk. Continue stirring over medium heat until mixture begins to thicken. Pour thickened milk into slow cooker. Add all remaining ingredients (except French bread). Cover with lid and cook on low 4-6 hours. Stir well before serving. Keep warm while serving. Dip French bread cubes into cheese to serve.

Good Time Party Dip

Prep. Time: less than 5 minutes • Serves: 6+ • Cost: about 41-cents per serving

2 pkgs. frozen chopped broccoli, thawed
1 can cream of mushroom soup
2 tubes Kraft Garlic-flavored cheese®

Combine all ingredients in slow cooker. Cover with lid and cook on low for 4-6 hours. Stir well before serving. Keep warm while serving. Serve with chips or crackers.

Cheese Ole Dip

Prep. Time: about 15 minutes • Serves: 6+ • Cost: about 43-cents per serving

2 lbs. American cheese, cubed
1 lb. lean ground beef or turkey, cooked and drained
1 medium onion, chopped
1 jar salsa (your choice on temperature)
1 can prepared chili without beans

In skillet, brown meat with chopped onion until done. Drain off all grease. Crumble meat into slow cooker. Add cheese cubes, salsa and chili. Cover with lid and cook on low for 6 hours. Stir to blend well before serving. Keep warm while serving. Use tortilla chips, corn chips or fresh vegetables to dip sauce.

Spicy Cheese Dip

Prep. Time: about 20 minutes • Serves: 6+ • Cost: about 61-cents per serving

1 lb. mild sausage
1 lb. hot sausage
2 cans cream of mushroom soup
1 lb. Mexican Velveeta® cheese, cubed
1 lb. American cheese, cubed
1 cup sour cream
1 tablespoon taco seasoning mix
2 cans green chilies, drained

In skillet, brown both sausages together until done. Drain meat and crumble into slow cooker. Add mushroom soup, cheese cubes, taco seasoning and green chilies. Cover with lid and cook on low for 4-6 hours. Add sour cream right before serving, stirring to blend well. Keep warm while serving.

Rueben Dip

Prep. Time: less than 5 minutes • Serves: 6+ • Cost: about 44-cents per serving

2 pkgs. (8 oz.) cream cheese
1 cup sour cream
2 cups drained sauerkraut, chopped
1 lb. cooked lean corned beef, chopped
1 onion, finely chopped
2 tablespoons ketchup
½ cup brown sugar, firmly packed
2 cups Swiss cheese, cubed
Serve with rye crackers

Combine cream cheese, sauerkraut, corned beef, onion, ketchup, and brown sugar in slow cooker. Cover with lid and cook on low for 4-6 hours. Add sour cream and Swiss cheese about an hour before ready to serve. Stir well before serving. Keep warm while serving.

SHRIMP COCKTAIL SAUCE

Prep. Time: about 5 minutes • Serves: 8+ • Cost: about 42-cents per serving

2 cups chili sauce
2 teaspoons horseradish
2 teaspoons Worcestershire sauce
1 teaspoon prepared mustard
½ teaspoon salt
1 teaspoon finely chopped onion
4 drops hot pepper sauce
2 teaspoons lemon juice

Combine all ingredients in slow cooker. Stir with a wire whisk to blend well. Cover with lid and cook on low for 4-6 hours. Serve warm or chilled with shrimp.

SWEDISH MEAT SAUCE

Prep. Time: less than 5 minutes • Serves: 8+ • Cost: about 27-cents per serving

2 cups of water
2 bottles of chili sauce
1 cup of BBQ Sauce
1 cup of grape jelly
1 cup of brown sugar

Mix all ingredients in slow cooker and cook on low for at least two hours before adding meats to sauce. Add cooked meatballs, sliced smoked sausage, mini-smoked sausage links, hot dogs, etc.

CREATIVE SERVING CONTAINERS

When inviting guests in for a meal, the presentation of the food goes hand-in-hand with its taste. For this reason, you'll want to take a little extra care in choosing the right serving containers. But you don't have to resort to renting serving trays or bowls from the local party-rental-supply-shop. Instead, get creative! Here are some suggestions:

• Use decorative containers you already have setting around your home such as the old-fashioned pitcher with wash basin. Fill the pitcher with a fruity punch and fill the basin with fruit salad. Use decorative cookie jars for soups or stews.

• Don't be afraid to mix and match different patterns and materials of serving containers. What used to be considered "hodge-podge" is now referred to as "shabby sheek" and is gaining in popularity for informal get-togethers. It's okay to use the stoneware bowls you got as a wedding gift along with your every-day Corelle (TM) bowls. You can even make use of your plastic mixing bowls! When using mix-and-match pieces, carrying the theme on by using a combination of wood or plastic handled flatware with silver-plated or sterling silver flatware, different styled cups or mugs, and a variety of plates in different patterns.

• Clean out empty flower pots (clay and/or plastic) and use those by first lining them with aluminum foil. Be sure to plug up the drainage holes before you line them. Get some small toy plastic shovels to use as spoons!

• If you've just remodeled and have empty paint cans, paint the outside of the cans in bright colors and line the inside with several layers of aluminum foil. Use clean wooden paint stirrers as accent pieces to stir soups, stews, etc.

• Save empty coffee cans and ice cream tubs. Decorate the outside of them with either paint, wallpaper, decoupage, or some other form of art and make sure the insides are clean. Use these as serving containers.

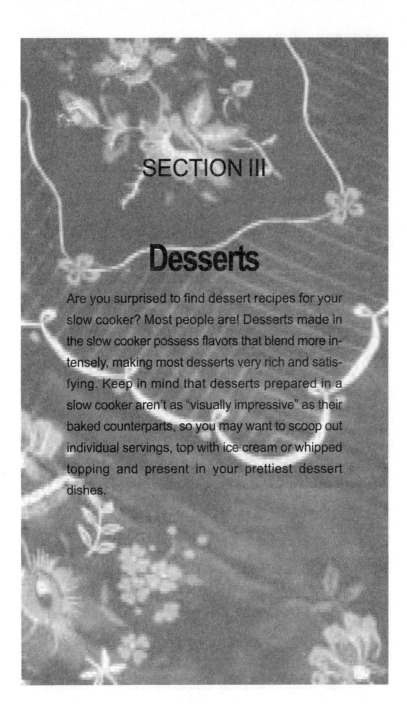

SECTION III

Desserts

Are you surprised to find dessert recipes for your slow cooker? Most people are! Desserts made in the slow cooker possess flavors that blend more intensely, making most desserts very rich and satisfying. Keep in mind that desserts prepared in a slow cooker aren't as "visually impressive" as their baked counterparts, so you may want to scoop out individual servings, top with ice cream or whipped topping and present in your prettiest dessert dishes.

BLUEBERRY DELIGHT

Prep. Time: about 5 minutes • Serves: 6 • Cost: about 35-cents per serving

½ stick butter or margarine, melted
1 cup sugar
1 cup Bisquick® or self-rising flour
1 cup milk
1 can prepared blueberry pie-filling fruit

Combine melted butter or margarine with sugar, Bisquick, ™ and milk in separate bowl. Pour into slow cooker. Pour canned fruit in center, do not stir. Cover top of slow cooker with a clean terry cloth kitchen towel and place lid over slow cooker. (Towel will help to absorb moisture.) Cook on high for 2-3 hours. Scoop out and serve with a dip of vanilla ice cream.

MAKE-AHEAD IDEAS

When planning a party, be kind to yourself by tackling as much as possible before the day of the event. You'll want to be well-rested and in good spirits when your guests arrive, not frazzled and stressed out! Here are some "do ahead" suggestions:

• If you're serving fruit tarts for dessert, do the shells or crusts ahead of time and freeze them. On the day of the event, simply take them out of the freezer, let thaw, and fill with fruit right before you're ready to serve. You don't want to fill these any too early as any juice from the fruit will soak into the crust and make them mushy.

• If you're going to serve ice cream sundaes for dessert, go ahead and dip the ice cream in advance. Form ice cream balls using your hands and set each ball on a cookie sheet. When you've filled the sheet, stick it in the freezer until the ice cream gets solid. On the day of the event, stick the ice cream glasses or containers in the refrigerator to chill them. When you're ready to serve, you'll "Wow!" your guests by serving uniform ice cream sundaes in a snap! Simply plop an ice cream ball in a glass, drizzle chocolate syrup over it, garnish with a mint leaf and a cherry and you're all set!

"Baked" Apples and Dumplings

Prep. Time: about 15 minutes • Serves: 8+ • Cost: about 49-cents per serving

5 - 6 lbs. tart apples, peeled and cored, sliced
4 ½ cups sugar
¼ cup cornstarch
1 tablespoon ground cinnamon
½ teaspoon nutmeg
1 teaspoon ground allspice
1 teaspoon salt
5 cups water
3 cups sweet apple cider or juice
2 cans refrigerator biscuits, 10 count

Combine all ingredients in slow cooker except for the biscuits. Cover with lid and cook on low for 4-5 hours. When apple slices are tender and liquid is thick and bubbly, remove lid. Cut each prepared refrigerator biscuit into quarters and drop into slow cooker. Stir to mix biscuits into apples. Cover slow cooker with a clean terry cloth kitchen towel and set lid over towel. (Towel will help absorb moisture.) Continue cooking for another hour. "Dumplings" will be doughy. Serve hot with a scoop of vanilla ice cream.

PEACH COBBLER

Prep. Time: about 10 minutes • Serves: 6+ • Cost: about 31-cents per serving

1 stick butter or margarine, melted
1 cup sugar
1 cup flour
2 teaspoons baking powder
¾ cup milk
2 cups sliced fresh or canned peaches
1 cup sugar

Pour melted butter or margarine into slow cooker and swirl around to coat bottom and sides. In bowl, combine 1 cup sugar, flour, baking powder and milk; beat on high with electric mixer. Pour flour mixture into slow cooker. Don't stir. Next, spoon peaches on top of flour mixture, then sprinkle with remaining sugar. Cover with a clean terry cloth kitchen towel and set lid over towel. (Towel will help absorb moisture.) Cook on low for 3-4 hours. Serve with vanilla ice cream or whipped topping.

Fresh Rhubarb Cobbler

Prep. Time: about 10 minutes • Serves: 6+ • Cost: about 36-cents per serving

4 cups fresh rhubarb, washed and diced
1¼ cups sugar
3 tablespoons butter or margarine, melted
2 eggs, beaten
2 teaspoons lemon juice
2 cups Bisquick®
1 cup sugar
½ cup brown sugar
½ cup milk
1½ teaspoons baking powder
½ teaspoon ground cinnamon

Combine cut rhubarb with 1¼ cups sugar, 3 tablespoons melted butter or margarine, lemon juice, and 2 eggs in bottom of slow cooker. Stir to mix well. In bowl, combine all remaining ingredients and mix well. Pour Bisquick mixture over fruit mixture. Do not stir. Cover with a clean terry cloth kitchen towel and set lid over towel. (Towel will help absorb moisture.) Cook on low for 3-4 hours.

STRAWBERRY RHUBARB DESSERT

Prep. Time: about 5 minutes • Serves: 6+ • Cost: about 34-cents per serving

5 cups finely chopped rhubarb
1 small box dry strawberry gelatin
1 cup sugar
½ cup butter or sugar, melted
2 eggs, beaten
1¾ cups boiling water
1 teaspoon salt
1¼ cups flour
2 tablespoons cornstarch

Combine all ingredients in slow cooker and stir to blend well. Cover with a clean terry cloth kitchen towel and set lid over towel. (Towel will help absorb moisture.) Cook on low for 3-4 hours. Remove slow cooker from heat source and let set for 1 hour before serving. This is especially good with ice cream or whipped cream.

YUMMY-GOOEY FRUITY DESSERT

Prep. Time: less than 5 minutes • Serves: 6+ • Cost: about 48-cents per serving

1 can pitted sour cherries, with juice (do not use cherry pie filling)
2 cups sugar
1 large can crushed pineapple, with juice
1 white or yellow cake mix
1 cup coconut
1 cup chopped pecans
1 cup melted butter

Pour cherries and pineapple in slow cooker. Sprinkle dry cake mix over fruit, but do not stir. Sprinkle coconut and chopped pecans over dry cake mix. Drizzle melted butter over all. Cover with a clean terry cloth kitchen towel and set lid over towel. (Towel will help absorb moisture.) Cook on low for 4-5 hours. Serve with ice cream or whipped cream.

CURRIED FRUIT

Prep. Time: about 10 minutes or less • Serves: 6+ • Cost: about 44-cents per serving

½ cup butter or margarine, melted
1¼ cups brown sugar, firmly packed
4 teaspoons curry powder
1 can pear halves, drained
½ cup maraschino cherries, drained
1 can sliced peaches, drained
1 can apricot halves, drained
1 can pineapple chunks, drained

Combine melted butter or margarine with brown sugar and curry powder. Cut pears, peaches, and apricots into bite-sized pieces. Add fruit to sugar-curry mixture and stir well to evenly coat. Pour into slow cooker. Cover with lid and cook on low for about 3 hours.

BAKED PEACH PUDDING

Prep. Time: about 15 minutes • Serves: 6+ • Cost: about 42-cents per serving

4 cups sliced raw peaches
2 cups sugar
1 cup brown sugar
1 pint Half and Half
½ stick butter or margarine
1 teaspoon baking powder
1 cup flour
1 tablespoon cornstarch
½ teaspoon salt
2 cups water

Prepare peaches and place sliced peaches (skins removed) in slow cooker. In separate bowl, combine sugar, brown sugar, baking powder, flour, and salt. Mix well. Melt butter and add to dry mixture. Add Half and Half and mix well until mixture forms a thick paste or dough. Dissolve cornstarch in 2 cups water and pour into dough mixture. Mix well. Pour over peaches and mix well to combine fruit with dough. Cover with a clean terry cloth kitchen towel and set lid over towel. (Towel will help absorb moisture.) Cook on low for 3-4 hours.

FRUIT COCKTAIL PUDDING

Prep. Time: about 10 minutes • Serves: 6+ • Cost: about 38-cents per serving

1½ cups flour
1 cup sugar
1 teaspoon baking soda
½ teaspoon salt
1 egg, slightly beaten
1 can fruit cocktail with juice (#2 can)
1 cup brown sugar
½ cup chopped nuts

Sift together flour with sugar, baking soda and salt. Add egg and beat to form a smooth batter. Add fruit cocktail with juice and blend well. Pour into greased slow cooker. Sprinkle brown sugar and chopped nuts over batter. Cover with a clean terry cloth kitchen towel and set lid over towel. (Towel will help absorb moisture.) Reduce heat to low and cook for 3-4 hours. Serve with ice cream or whipped cream.

BAKED RHUBARB PUDDING

Prep. Time: about 15 minutes • Serves: 6+ • Cost: about 33-cents per serving

6 cups raw rhubarb, cut in slices
2 cups sugar
1 cup brown sugar
1 teaspoon nutmeg
2 teaspoons ground cinnamon
1 pint Half and Half
1 stick butter or margarine, melted
1 teaspoon baking powder
1 cup flour
1 tablespoon cornstarch
½ teaspoon salt
2 cups water

Wash stalks of rhubarb and slice. In separate bowl, combine sugar, brown sugar, baking powder, flour, cinnamon, nutmeg and salt. Mix well. Melt butter or margarine and add to dry mixture. Add Half and Half and mix well until mixture forms a thick paste or dough. Dissolve cornstarch in 2 cups water and pour into dough mixture. Mix well. Add fresh rhubarb and mix well to combine fruit with dough. Pour all into slow cooker. Cover with a clean terry cloth kitchen towel and set lid over towel. (Towel will help absorb moisture.) Cook on low for 4-5 hours. Stir before serving.

BAKED APPLE PUDDING

Prep. Time: about 15 minutes • Serves: 8+ • Cost: about 38-cents per serving

6 cups tart apples, cored and peeled, sliced
1½ cups sugar
½ cup brown sugar
1 tablespoon ground cinnamon
½ teaspoon nutmeg
¼ teaspoon ground ginger
1 pint Half and Half
1 stick butter or margarine
1 teaspoon baking powder
1 cup flour
1 tablespoon cornstarch
½ teaspoon salt
2 cups water

Peel and core apples. Slice into slow cooker. In separate bowl, combine sugars with cinnamon, nutmeg, ginger, baking powder, flour and salt. Mix well. Melt butter and add to dry mixture. Stir in Half and Half. Dissolve cornstarch in 2 cups water and add to flour mixture. Stir to mix well. Add to slow cooker and stir to blend fruit with pasty-dough mixture. Cover with a clean terry cloth kitchen towel and set lid over towel. (Towel will help absorb moisture.) Cook on low for 4-5 hours. Stir before serving.

CREAMY FUDGE SAUCE

Prep. Time: less than 5 minutes • Serves: 6+ • Cost: about 35-cents per serving

4 tablespoons butter
2 small pkgs. (6 oz.) chocolate chips
2 cans sweetened condensed milk
2 teaspoons vanilla
¼ teaspoon salt

Combine all ingredients in slow cooker. Turn heat setting on high and cook without lid for 4 hours. Stir occasionally. Serve over ice cream.

HOT FUDGE TAPIOCA SAUCE

Prep. Time: about 5 minutes • Serves: 8+ • Cost: about 11-cents per serving

2 cups sugar
¼ cup plus 1 tablespoon cocoa
½ stick butter or margarine, melted
2 cups 2% or whole milk
2 teaspoons vanilla
3 tablespoons tapioca pearls

In blender combine milk with cocoa and mix on medium speed for about 15 seconds. Pour into slow cooker. Add remaining ingredients to slow cooker. Stir to mix well. Cover with clean terry cloth towel, then set lid on top. Cook on low for 3-4 hours. Stir before serving. Use this sauce over fudge cake, brownies or ice cream.

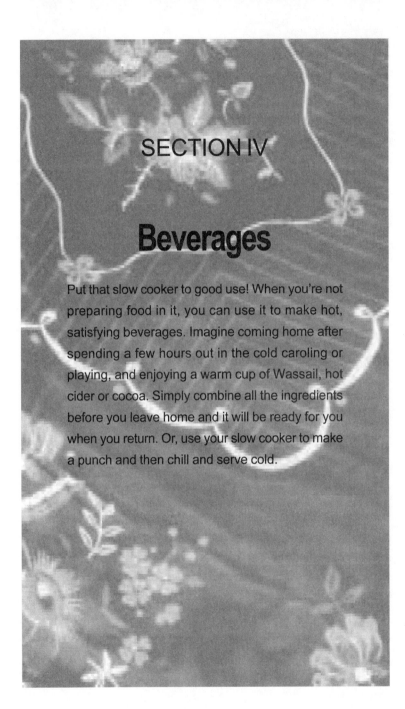

SECTION IV

Beverages

Put that slow cooker to good use! When you're not preparing food in it, you can use it to make hot, satisfying beverages. Imagine coming home after spending a few hours out in the cold caroling or playing, and enjoying a warm cup of Wassail, hot cider or cocoa. Simply combine all the ingredients before you leave home and it will be ready for you when you return. Or, use your slow cooker to make a punch and then chill and serve cold.

APPLE BREW

Prep. Time: less than 5 minutes • Serves: 6+ • Cost: about 12-cents per serving

4 cups apple juice
4 cups water
1 pkg. red Kool Aid®
1 cup sugar
4 cinnamon sticks
5 whole cloves

Combine all ingredients in slow cooker. Turn on high and cover with lid. Cook for 2 hours. Remove whole cloves and cinnamon sticks before serving. Reduce heat to low and serve directly from the slow cooker. Or chill and pour into a punch bowl and serve.

HOT CIDER

Prep. Time: less than 5 minutes • Serves: 6+ • Cost: about 16-cents per serving

1 jug (46 oz.) sweet apple cider
4 cinnamon sticks, about 2-3-inches long
¼ cup honey
1 cup pineapple juice
3 whole cloves
¼ cup lemon juice

Combine all ingredients in slow cooker. Turn on high and cover with lid. Cook for 2 hours. Remove whole cloves and cinnamon sticks before serving. Reduce heat to low and serve directly from the slow cooker.

Hot Cranberry Delight

Prep. Time: less than 5 minutes • Serves: 6+ • Cost: about 17-cents per serving

4 cups cranberry juice
2 cups apple juice
2 cups orange juice
½ cup maple-flavored syrup
4 cinnamon sticks, about 2-3-inches long
3 whole cloves

Combine all ingredients in slow cooker. Turn on high and cover with lid. Cook for 2 hours. Remove whole cloves and cinnamon stick before serving. Reduce heat to low and serve directly from the slow cooker.

Hot Cranapple Punch

Prep. Time: less than 5 minutes • Serves: 8+ • Cost: about 18-cents per serving

1 gallon Cranapple drink
2 cans (46 oz.) apple juice
2 cans (46 oz.) Hi-C Apple® drink
10 cinnamon sticks, each about 2-inches long
20 whole cloves, tied in cheesecloth
2/3 cup brown sugar

Wrap cinnamon sticks and cloves in cheesecloth and tie off. Combine all ingredients in slow cooker. Turn on low and let simmer for a minimum of 3 hours. Remove cheesecloth and stir before serving.

Honey-Cinnamon Wassail

Prep. Time: about 10 minutes • Servings: 6 • Cost: about 14-cents per serving

6 cups apple cider
2 cinnamon sticks
¼ teaspoon nutmeg
½ cup honey
2 tablespoons lemon juice
1 can (1 lb. 4 oz) unsweetened pineapple juice

Combine apple cider and cinnamon sticks first. Cover with lid and simmer on high for 3 hours. Add remaining ingredients and turn temperature setting to low. May begin serving after simmering on low for an additional 2 hours.

Sugar 'n' Spice

Prep. Time: less than 5 minutes • Serves: 8+ • Cost: about 18-cents per serving

1 cup brown sugar, heaping
½ teaspoon salt
1 quart cranberry juice
1 quart apple juice
½ cup lemon juice
1 cup sugar
2 teaspoons whole allspice
2 teaspoon whole cloves
3 sticks cinnamon

Combine all ingredients in slow cooker. Turn on low and cover with lid. Cook for at least 3 hours before serving. Remove whole cloves, allspice and cinnamon sticks when ready to serve. Serve directly from the slow cooker.

PERKY PUNCH

Prep. Time: about 5 minutes • Serves: 8+ • Cost: about 20 cents per serving

2 quarts cranberry juice
2 large cans (46 oz.) pineapple juice
1 quart water
¾ cup brown sugar
2 fresh lemons, quartered
1 tablespoon whole allspice
4 ½ teaspoons whole cloves
4 sticks cinnamon, broken in pieces
½ teaspoon salt

Pour cranberry juice, pineapple juice and water in slow cooker. In a large square of cheesecloth, combine brown sugar, fresh lemons, allspice, cloves, cinnamon and salt. Tie cheesecloth with a piece of clean string and drop cheesecloth bundle into slow cooker. Cover with lid and cook on low for at least 3 - 4 hours. Remove cheesecloth before serving. Punch may be served warm directly from the slow cooker or chilled from a punch bowl.

CINNAMON CRAN-PINEAPPLE PUNCH

Prep. Time: about 5 minutes • Serves: 8+ • Cost: about 22-cents per serving

2 large cans unsweetened pineapple punch
9 cups cranberry cocktail juice
4¼ cups water
1 cup brown sugar
1 heaping tablespoon whole cloves
4 cinnamon sticks, broken in pieces
¼ teaspoon salt

In a double-layered piece of cheesecloth, combine brown sugar, whole cloves, cinnamon stick pieces and salt. Pull ends up and secure with a rubber band or twist tie. Drop spices in cheesecloth in slow cooker. Add remaining ingredients. Turn slow cooker on high and cook for 3 hours or longer. Reduce heat to low and serve punch warm. Or chill punch and serve from a punch bowl.

SWEET RED PUNCH

2 pkgs. cherry Kool-Aid®
1 pkg. strawberry Kool-Aid®
5 cups sugar
4 quarts water
1 can (12 oz.) concentrated orange juice, thawed
1 can (46 oz.) unsweetened pineapple juice
1 can (46 oz.) grapefruit juice

Combine Kool-Aid® with sugar and enough water to make a paste. Let this set for about 10 minutes. Combine remaining ingredients in slow cooker. Add sugar-paste and stir to dissolve. Cover with lid and cook on low for 4-6 hours. Serve warm or over ice.

MISTLETOE PUNCH

Prep. Time: about 5 minutes • Serves: 8+ • Cost: about 17-cents per serving

10 cups cranberry juice cocktail
5 cups orange juice
4 cups water
1 1/3 cups sugar
6 cinnamon sticks, broken in pieces
3 whole oranges, peeled and cut into wedges
½ teaspoon nutmeg
8 teaspoons instant tea powder
skewered whole fresh cranberries

Combine cranberry juice, orange juice, water, sugar, cinnamon, nutmeg, and oranges in slow cooker. Turn on high and bring to a boil. Stir in tea when mixture is boiling hot. Add skewered cranberries. Reduce heat to low and keep warm. Serve as desired either warm from the slow cooker or chilled over ice.

HOT SPICED TEA

Prep. Time: about 15 minutes • Serves: 8+ • Cost: about 12-cents per serving

4 quarts water
6 decaf. tea bags (single cup sized tea bags)
2 cups sugar
Juice of 3 oranges
Zest from 3 oranges
Juice of 2 lemons
Zest from 2 lemons
1 tablespoon whole cloves
4 cinnamon sticks

Combine water, sugar, and fruit juices in slow cooker. Turn slow cooker on low. In cheesecloth combine cloves, cinnamon sticks, orange zest, and lemon zest. Tie off and set in slow cooker. Simmer this mixture a minimum of 3 hours. When almost ready to serve, add tea bags and let steep 15 minutes. Remove tea bags and cheesecloth and serve.

HAWAIIAN TEA

1 cup boiling water
1 cup sugar
1 can (yield 2 quarts) frozen lemon juice concentrate, thawed
1 large can (46 oz.) unsweetened pineapple juice
2 quarts freshly brewed black or green tea
1 (8 oz.) bottle maraschino cherries with syrup

Combine boiling water and sugar in slow cooker and stir until sugar is dissolved. Combine all remaining ingredients and stir to blend well. Cover and cook on low for 4 hours. Serve by pouring over crushed ice and serve cold. Each glass should get at least one cherry!

BRAZILIAN COFFEE

Prep. Time: about 5 minutes • Serves: 8+ • Cost: about 13-cents per serving

1/3 cup cocoa
1 tablespoon instant coffee (dry powder)
½ teaspoon salt
3 cinnamon sticks
1 can sweetened condensed milk
6½ cups water

In slow cooker, combine cocoa, coffee, salt and cinnamon sticks. Add the sweetened condensed milk and stir to blend well. Turn slow cooker on high and stir occasionally as mixture heats up. When mixture is hot, but not boiling, slowly add in water, stirring well after each addition. Continue cooking coffee in slow cooker until it is hot and you=re ready to serve it. To keep it at the right drinking temperature over an extended period of time, reduce heat to low after adding water. Remove cinnamon sticks before serving.

BRAZILIAN HOT CHOCOLATE

Prep. Time: about 5 minutes • Serves: 8 • Cost: about 22-cents per serving

2/3 cup cocoa
1 cup sugar
2 tablespoons instant coffee granules
3 cinnamon sticks
½ teaspoon salt
2 cups hot tap water
7 cups milk
2 teaspoons vanilla

In slow cooker combine cocoa, sugar, instant coffee, salt and cinnamon sticks. Blend in hot tap water and stir to blend well. Turn slow cooker on low and heat mixture until hot, but not boiling. Add milk, stirring after each cup is added. Let hot cocoa blend for 2-3 hours before serving. When you=re ready to serve, remove cinnamon sticks and add vanilla. With an electric mixer, beat the cocoa on low speed in order to create a frothy foam on top. Serve immediately.

GO ORGANIC

When offering your guests a dip for their vegetables, try these ready-made containers:

• Green, red, orange, and yellow bell peppers: remove core and seeds and use upright or slice in half and fill each side.

• Hollow out a head of cabbage and use it for dip.

• Hollow out large tomatoes, remove core, and "decorate" by cutting a jagged edge border. Fill with dip.

• Use your choice of squash by cutting in half and hollowing out the flesh and seeds. Doing this with uncooked squash can be difficult due to the squash being so hard to cut through. You may want to go ahead and bake the squash until tender, then cut it in half and scoop out the flesh and seeds. Just use caution when filling to make sure the remaining rind will hold its contents without spilling or oozing.

SPICY TOMATO JUICE

Prep. Time: about 15 minutes • Serves: 8 • Cost: about 14-cents per serving

2 medium onions, chopped
4 stalks celery, chopped
4 whole cloves
2 bay leaves
2 quarts tomato juice
1 cup sugar
2 tablespoons salt
½ teaspoon black pepper
½ teaspoon ground cinnamon
1 teaspoon Worcestershire sauce
1 quart water

Combine chopped celery, cloves, and bay leaves with 1 quart water in slow cooker. Cover and cook on high for 2 hours. Add tomato juice, sugar, salt, pepper, cinnamon and Worcestershire sauce. Cover and continue cooking on high for 2-4 more hours. Pour all contents through colander, and discard vegetables. Serve drained spicy tomato juice either warm or chilled.

TOMATO BOUILLON

Prep. Time: about 10 minutes • Serves: 8+ • Cost: about 19-cents per serving

4 quarts tomato juice
1 large onion, left whole
4 bay leaves
2 teaspoons oregano
2 teaspoons seasoned salt
½ teaspoon black pepper
1 teaspoon celery seed
2/3 cup brown sugar

Combine all ingredients in slow cooker. Cover with lid and cook on low for 6 hours. Remove onion from slow cooker with½ cup liquid and put in blender. Add ½ cup cold water and puree onion with juice. Return pureed onion to slow cooker. Remove bay leaves and discard. Stir before serving. This can be served either warm or chilled.

HOT TOMATO PUNCH

Prep. Time: about 5 minutes • Serves: 8+ • Cost: about 19-cents per serving

2 quarts tomato juice
2 cans (10.5 oz) condensed beef consomme
2 teaspoons grated onion
2 teaspoons horseradish
¼ teaspoon pepper
2 teaspoons Worcestershire sauce
2 whole lemons, sliced and seeded
whole cloves

In slow cooker, combine tomato juice with beef consomme, grated onion, horseradish, pepper, and Worcestershire sauce. Stir to blend well. Turn slow cooker on high and cover with lid. Let mixture cook for 2 hours. Stick whole cloves in lemon slices and add those to the slow cooker when ready to serve. To keep warm, reduce heat to low and serve as desired.

About The Author:

Penny E. Stone and her husband enjoy invit-
ing friends and family into their home for a
meal and social get-together. Sometimes she
even has three slow cookers going at once!
"With all of our hectic schedules, it's not easy
to find the time to entertain anymore, but with
slow cookers it does become easier. I've dis-
covered by putting my slow cookers to use I'm
less stressed and frazzled when I do decide

to invite company over. By cooking with slow cookers, I don't need to
worry about my food not turning out or burning. For me, cooking in a
slow cooker is the one sure way to guarantee success!" Penny and her
family reside in central Indiana. When she's not entertaining or work-
ing on her writing career, Penny enjoys being involved in the lives of
her three children, assisting her husband run a home-based busi-
ness, gardening, and being active in her church.

INDEX

LIFESTYLE SOLUTIONS